GOD.COM

Inspirational Impact

GOD.COM

Inspirational Impact

S Clarke

you will be blessed

Compiled and Edited by

Albert A. C. Waite PhD

[signature]

11 Jun 2003

MANDRA PUBLISHING

First published in 2003 by
Mandra Publishing
P.O. Box 5136
Riseley
RG7 1GT

ISBN 0-9540429-3-X

A catalogue record for this book is available from the British Library.

Printed and bound in Great Britain by
Bookcraft
Midsomer Norton
Bath, BA3 4BS

This book is dedicated to the three people who
know me most: EIW and AACW^2

BENEFICIARY

The profit from the sale of this book will benefit
The Cold Spring Basic School at Garlands,
St. James, Jamaica.

Message from the Headteacher:

We thank you, the reader, for purchasing this book
to help the children at our little school to get a
good start on their educational ladder. We are
grateful to Dr Albert A C Waite who, for many
years, has contributed computers and educational
material to our school.

Mrs Elvie Anderson-Reid
February 2003

COMMENTS

A few things struck me about GOD.COM. The combination of true stories, testimonies and poems are spiritually stimulating and inspiring. They offer a young Christian the encouragement they need to lead a life in Christ.

Some stories are easy to relate to, others are truly amazing examples of miracles, all of which have happened to normal people who put their faith in God. I would recommend this book to anyone looking for some spiritual encouragement.

Claire Lowry
Ireland

If all books were this good, there would be no need for public libraries. GOD.COM inspires the reader and helps us to remember the important things in life: love, connections and gratitude. Our lives are full of emotions and this book seems to touch them all. It helps us to remember that our actions and words not only affect us but those we come in contact with. A great read for all age groups.

Duane C. Saunders
Wales

A truly inspirational book, full of pearl drops of wisdom encased in clouds of light humour. This collection is bursting with thoughts that you just want to remember and share with others.

The stories are short and provocative, mentally stimulating and challenging; whilst the poetry strikes a wonderful equilibrium between brevity and detail. This

book is really where its @! It struck a chord within me. One word, touching!
Andreas Beccai
Reading

The book is inspirational and motivational. As you turn the pages, you are captivated with anticipation; as you read, you are on the cerebral edge of expectancy; as you digest, you are filled with delight and wanting more!
Dr Richard De Lisser
London

'Inspirational Impact' is an appropriate description for this book. This collection of stories, prayers, poems and thoughts is simple and easy to understand; yet it has many thought-provoking and powerful messages. It will inspire and encourage all types of people from all ages, cultures and backgrounds. It is a message of hope, joy, happiness and most of all, our loving Saviour, Jesus Christ. GOD.COM will strengthen the faith of any Christian, and appeal to those who do not know Jesus.
Daniel Edwards
Scotland

ACKNOWLEDGEMENTS

They keep coming: stories, poems, prayers and
thoughts. Twenty-four-seven they come. They come
with the same implied message: 'Share this with as
many people as you can.'

Then I thought, there are many people who do not have
the Internet, how will they know of these gems? And
there is the need of that little school which I attended as
an under-seven. What a combination. Inspiration?
Maybe.

So firstly I must thank all those Internet wizards who
thought to share with me the pearls they received.
Some regularly: Simeon Esson, Jackie F. Johnson,
Colin Samuels, Blossom Thomas and Annette
Robinson; others less frequent: Ullanda Alexander,
Icylin Brown, Marlon Jones, Michael Mannix and
Gifford Rhamie. Also to those whose names I did not
save. Every e-contribution is treasured.

Much appreciation is due to Alicia A C Waite, who
serves magnificently as assistant editor, and to my
at-home family, to whom this book is dedicated. To
Greg Wilson, who transformed an idea into a cover.

The enthusiasm captured by the diverse readers of the
manuscript is encouraging. And finally, but most
significantly, to all the unknown authors who send out
their work on the Internet; your creation is being used
to help many people and hopefully those children at
that little country school in Garlands, Jamaica.

Thank you everyone.

CONTENTS

FROM THE EDITOR...

As the reader will realise by now, GOD.COM is a compilation of stories, poems, prayers and thoughts that were sent to me on the Internet. The endings of each item had a message encouraging the reader to send it on to other Internet users.

These endings have been removed and, in many cases, the bodies of the texts have been extensively changed. Also, different titles are attributed to some pieces, where it was felt that these would convey a more meaningful message.

It is felt that this strong inspirational and motivational compilation, GOD.COM, will encourage every reader of any age group to seek and appreciate God, the Creator of our Universe, as He works His purpose out in our lives, if we let Him.

The power of GOD.COM is twofold: each of the many authors, even though unknown, must have been inspired by God, and, the text is in simple, uncomplicated language making it accessible to all readers, thus conveying its profound message in a powerful way.

No one should be disappointed.

AACW
Conifers
Three Mile Cross
March 2003

GOOD MORNING

I am God. Today, I will be handling all your problems. Please remember that I do not need your help.

If the devil happens to deliver a situation to you that you cannot handle, DO NOT attempt to resolve it. Kindly put it in the SFJTD (something for Jesus to do) box. It will be addressed in MY time, not yours.

Once the matter is placed in the box, DO NOT hold on to it or attempt to remove it. Holding on or removal will delay the resolution of your problem.

If it is a situation that you think you are capable of handling, please consult me in prayer, to be sure that it is the proper resolution.

Because I do not sleep nor do I slumber, there is no need for you to lose any sleep. Rest my child. If you need to contact me, I am only a prayer away.

STORIES

A GLASS OF MILK

One day, a poor boy, who was selling goods from door to door to pay his way through school, found he had only one thin dime left, and he was hungry. He decided that he would ask for a meal at the next house.

However, he lost his nerve when a lovely young woman opened the door. Instead of a meal, he asked for a drink of water. She thought he looked hungry, so she brought him a large glass of milk. He drank it slowly and then asked, "How much do I owe you?"

"You don't owe me anything," she replied. "Mother has taught us never to accept pay for a kindness."

He said, "Then I thank you from my heart." As Howard Kelly left that house, he not only felt stronger physically, but his faith in God and humankind was strong, also. He had been ready to give up.

Years later, that young woman became critically ill. The local doctors were baffled. They finally sent her to the big city, where they called in specialists to study her rare disease. Dr. Howard Kelly was called in for the consultation. When he heard the name of the town she came from, a strange light filled his eyes. Immediately, he rose and went down the hall of the hospital to her room.

Dressed in his doctor's gown, he went in to see her. He recognised her at once. He went back to the consultation room, determined to do his best to save her life. And from that day, he gave special attention to the case.

After a long struggle, the battle was won. Dr. Kelly requested the business office to pass the final bill to him for approval. He looked at it, then wrote something on the edge, and the bill was sent to her room. She feared to open it, for she was sure it would take the rest of her life to pay for it all. Finally she looked, and something caught her attention on the side of the bill. She read these words,

Paid in full with one glass of milk.

 Dr. Howard Kelly.

Tears of joy flooded her eyes, as her happy heart prayed:
"Thank You, God, that Your love has spread abroad, through human hearts and hands."

JOHN 3:16

In the city of Chicago, one cold, dark night, a blizzard was setting in. A little boy was selling newspapers on the corner, but he was so cold that he wasn't trying to sell many.

He walked up to a policeman and said, "Mister, you wouldn't happen to know where a poor boy could find a warm place to sleep tonight would you? You see, I sleep in a box down the alley there and it's awfully cold in there tonight. It would be nice to have a warm place to stay."

The policeman looked down at the little boy and said, "You go down the street to that big white house and knock on the door. When they open the door, just say, John 3:16, and they will let you in."

Reaching the white house, he walked up the steps and knocked on the door. A lady answered. He looked up and said, "John 3:16."
The lady said, "Come on in, son."

She took him in and sat him down in a split bottom rocker in front of a great big old fireplace, and she went off. The boy sat there for a while and thought to himself: *John 3:16....I don't understand it, but it sure makes a cold boy warm.*

Later she came back and asked him, "Are you hungry?" He said, "Well, just a little. I haven't eaten in a couple of days, and I guess I would like a little bit of food." The lady took him in the kitchen and sat him down to a table full of wonderful food. He ate until he couldn't eat any more. Then he thought to himself: *John 3:16... Boy, I sure don't understand it but it sure makes a hungry boy full.*

She took him upstairs to a bathroom to a huge bathtub filled with warm water, and he sat there and soaked for a while. He thought to himself: *John 3:16... I don't understand it, but it sure makes a dirty boy clean. You know, I've not had a bath, a real bath, in my whole life. The only bath I ever had was when I stood in front of that big, old fire hydrant as they flushed it out.*

The lady came in and got him. She took him to a room, tucked him into a big, old feather bed, pulled the covers up around his neck, kissed him goodnight and turned out the lights. As he lay in the darkness and looked out the window at the snow coming down on that cold night, he thought to himself: *John 3:16... I don't understand it, but it sure provides comfort for a tired boy.*

The next morning, the lady came back up and took him down again to that big table full of food. After he ate, she took him back to that big, old split bottom rocker in front of the fireplace, and picked

24

up a big, old Bible. She sat down in front of him and looked into his young face.

"Do you understand John 3:16?" she asked gently. He replied, "No, Ma'am, I don't. The first time I ever heard it was last night when the policeman told me to use it." She opened the Bible to John 3:16 and began to explain to him about Jesus. Right there, in front of that big, old fireplace, he gave his heart and life to Jesus. He sat there and thought: *John 3:16... I don't understand it, but it sure makes a lost boy feel safe.*

You know, I have to confess I don't understand it either, how God was willing to send His Son to die for me, and how Jesus would agree to do such a thing. I don't understand the agony of the Father and every angel in heaven as they watched Jesus suffer and die. I don't understand the intense love for me that kept Jesus on the cross 'till the end. I don't understand it, but it sure does make life worth living.

ATTITUDE

Michael was the kind of guy you love to hate. He was always in a good mood and always had something positive to say.

When someone would ask him how he was doing, he would reply, "If I were any better, I would be twins!"

He was a natural motivator.

If an employee was having a bad day, Michael would be there, telling the employee how to look on the positive side of the situation.

Seeing this style really made me curious. So one day, I went up to Michael and asked him, "I don't get it! You can't be a positive person all of the time. How do you do it?"

Michael replied, "Each morning I wake up and say to myself, you have two choices today: You can choose to be in a good mood or you can choose to be in a bad mood. I choose to be in a good mood.

"Each time something bad happens, I can choose to be a victim or I can choose to learn from it. I choose to learn from it.

"Every time someone comes to me complaining, I can choose to accept their complaining or I can point out the positive side of life. I choose the positive side of life."

"Yeah, right, it's not that easy," I protested. "Yes, it is," Michael said. "Life is all about choices. When you cut away all the junk, in every situation there is a choice.

"You choose how you react to situations. You choose how people affect your mood. You choose to be in a good mood or bad mood. The bottom line is: It's your choice how you live your life."

I reflected on what Michael said.

Soon thereafter, I left the Tower Industry to start my own business. We lost touch, but I often thought about him when I made a choice about life instead of reacting to it.

Several years later, I heard that Michael was involved in a serious accident, falling some 60 feet from a communications tower.

After 18 hours of surgery and weeks of intensive care, Michael was released from the hospital with rods placed in his back.

I saw Michael about six months after the accident. When I asked him how he was, he replied, "If I were any better, I'd be twins. Wanna see my scars?"

I declined to see his wounds, but I did ask him what had gone through his mind as the accident took place.

"The first thing that went through my mind was the well-being of my soon-to-be-born daughter," Michael replied. "Then, as I lay on the ground, I remembered that I had two choices: I could choose to live or I could choose to die. I chose to live."

"Weren't you scared? Did you lose consciousness?" I asked. Michael continued, "The paramedics were great. They kept telling me I was going to be fine. But, when they wheeled me into the ER and I saw the expressions on the faces of the doctors and nurses, I got really scared. In their eyes, I read, "He's a dead man." I knew I needed to take action."

"What did you do?" I asked.
"Well, there was a big burly nurse shouting questions at me," said Michael. "She asked if I was allergic to anything.
"Yes," I replied. The doctors and nurses stopped working as they waited for my reply. I took a deep breath and yelled, "Gravity." Over their laughter, I told them, "I am choosing to live. Operate on me as if I am alive, not dead."

Michael lived, thanks to the skill of his doctors, but also because of his amazing attitude. I learned from him that, every day, we have the choice to live fully.

Attitude, after all, is everything.

Therefore, do not worry about tomorrow, for tomorrow will worry about itself. Each day has enough trouble of its own. *Matthew 6:34*

After all, today is the tomorrow you worried about yesterday.

GOD'S PERFECTION

In Brooklyn, New York, CHUSH is a school that caters for children with learning disabilities. Some children remain in CHUSH for their entire school career, while others can be mainstreamed into conventional schools.

At a CHUSH fund-raising dinner, the father of a CHUSH child delivered a speech that would never be forgotten by all who attended.

After extolling the school and its dedicated staff, he cried out, "Where is the perfection in my son, Shay? Everything God does is done with perfection. But my child cannot understand things as other children do. My child cannot remember facts and figures, as other children do. Where is God's perfection?"

The audience was shocked by the question, pained by the father's anguish and stilled by the piercing query. "I believe," the father answered, "that when God brings a child like this into the world, the perfection that He seeks is in the way people react to this child."

He then told the following story about his son, Shay:
 One afternoon, Shay and his father walked past a park where some boys, who Shay knew, were

playing baseball. Shay asked, "Do you think they will let me play?" Shay's father knew that his son was not at all athletic and that most boys would not want him on their team. But Shay's father understood that if his son was chosen to play, it would give him a comfortable sense of belonging.

Shay's father approached one of the boys in the field and asked if Shay could play. The boy looked around for guidance from his team-mates.

Getting none, he took matters into his own hands and said, "We are losing by six runs and the game is in the eighth inning. I guess he can be on our team and we'll try to put him up to bat in the ninth inning."

Shay's father was ecstatic as Shay smiled broadly. Shay was told to put on a glove and go out to play short centre field. In the bottom of the eighth inning, Shay's team scored a few runs but was still behind by three.

In the bottom of the ninth inning, Shay's team scored again and now with two outs and the bases loaded with the potential winning run on base, Shay was scheduled to be up. Would the team actually let Shay bat at this juncture and give away their chance to win the game?

Surprisingly, Shay was given the bat. Everyone knew that it was all but impossible because Shay didn't even know how to hold the bat properly, let alone hit with it. As Shay stepped up to the plate, the pitcher moved a few steps to lob the ball in softly, so Shay should at least be able to make contact.

The first pitch came and Shay swung clumsily and missed. One of Shay's team-mates came up to Shay and together they held the bat and faced the pitcher waiting for the next pitch. The pitcher again took a few steps forward to toss the ball softly toward Shay. As the pitch came in, Shay and his team-mate swung at the ball and together they hit a slow ground ball to the pitcher.

The pitcher picked up the soft grounder and could easily have thrown the ball to the first baseman. Shay would have been out and that would have ended the game. Instead, the pitcher took the ball and threw it on a high arc to right field, far beyond reach of the first baseman.

Everyone started yelling, "Shay, run to first! Run to first!" Never in his life had Shay run to first. He scampered down the baseline, wide-eyed and startled. By the time he reached first base, the right fielder had the ball. He could have thrown the ball to the second baseman who would tag out Shay, who was still running. But the right fielder understood what the pitcher's intentions were, so he threw the ball high and far over the third baseman's head.

Everyone yelled, "Run to second, run to second."
Shay ran towards second base as the runners ahead
of him deliriously circled the bases towards home.

As Shay reached second base, the opposing short
stop ran to him, turned him in the direction of third
base and shouted, "Run to third." As Shay rounded
third, the boys from both teams ran behind him
screaming, "Shay run home."

Shay ran home, stepped on home plate and all 18
boys lifted him on their shoulders and made him
the hero, as he had just hit a 'grand slam' and won
the game for his team.

"That day," said the father softly, with tears now
rolling down his face, "those 18 boys reached their
level of God's perfection."

JESUS AT THE WINDOW

A little boy and his sister visited their grandparents on their farm. He was given a slingshot to play with in the woods. He practiced, but couldn't hit the target. Becoming discouraged, he headed back to dinner. As he walked back, he saw Grandma's pet duck. Out of impulse, he let the slingshot fly, hit the duck square in the head, and killed it. He was shocked. In a panic, he hid the dead duck in the woodpile, only to see his sister watching. Sally had seen it all, but she said nothing.

After lunch that day Grandma said, "Sally, let's wash the dishes."
But Sally said, "Grandma, Johnny told me he wanted to help in the kitchen."
Then Sally whispered to him, "Remember the duck?" So Johnny did the dishes.

Later that day, Grandpa asked if the children wanted to go fishing. Grandma said, "I'm sorry, but I need Sally to help make supper."
Sally smiled and said, "Well that's all right because Johnny told me he wanted to help make supper."
Sally whispered again to Johnny, "Remember the duck?" So Sally went fishing with Grandpa and Johnny stayed to help Grandma make supper.

After several days of Johnny doing his chores and those of Sally, he could stand it no longer. He came to Grandma and confessed that he had killed the duck. Grandma knelt beside Johnny and said, "I know. I was standing at the window and I saw the whole thing. Because I love you, I forgave you. I was just wondering how long you would let Sally make a slave of you."

Thought For The Day: Whatever is in your past, whatever you have done that the enemy throws in your face (lying, cheating, gossiping, debt, fear, hatred, anger, un-forgiveness, bitterness, backbiting, slander, stealing, etc.), whatever it is, Jesus Christ was standing at the window and saw the whole thing. He wants you to know that He loves you and that you are forgiven. He wonders how long you will let the enemy make a slave of you. Remember, God not only forgives you, He forgets!

Be kind, for everyone you meet is fighting some sort of difficult battle. It may not be named above, but Jesus is at the window of the battle!

CLOSED DOORS

We need to learn to thank the Lord for closed doors, as we do an open door. The reason God closes doors is because He has not prepared anything through them for us. If he didn't close the wrong door we would never find our way to the right one. Even when we don't realise it, God directs our paths through the closing and opening of doors.

When one door closes, it forces us to change our course. When another door closes, it forces us to change our course, yet again. Then finally, we find the open door and walk right into our blessing. But instead of praising God for the closed doors (which kept us out of trouble), we get upset because we judge by the appearances. And, in our own arrogance, or ignorance, we insist that we know what is right.

We have a very present help in the time of need – He is always standing guard. Because He walks ahead of us, He can see trouble down the road and sets up roadblocks and detours accordingly.

But, through our lack of wisdom we try to tear down the roadblocks or push aside the detour signs. Then, the minute we get into trouble, we start crying, "Lord how could this happen to me?" We have got to realise that the closed door was a blessing. Did He not say, "No good thing will He withhold from them that love him?"

If you get terminated from your job, don't be down for too long. Thank God for the new opportunities that will manifest themselves – it might be a better job, or an opportunity to go to school.

If that man or woman won't return your call, it might not be them. It might be the Lord setting up a roadblock (just let it go).

One time a person had a bank that he had been doing business with for many years, refuse him a £10,000 loan. The Lord led him to call another bank. That bank approved a £40,000 loan for him, at a lower interest rate than his own bank had advertised.

I'm so grateful for the many times God has closed doors for me, just to open others in the most unexpected places.

The steps of a good man are ordered by the Lord, and He delights in his way.

Psalm 37:23

§

The Mountain top is glorious, but it is in the Valley that I will grow!

Always remember, God gives you . . .
· Enough Happiness to keep you Sweet
· Enough Trials to keep you Strong
· Enough Sorrows to keep you Human
· Enough Hope to keep you Happy
· Enough Failure to keep you Humble
· Enough Success to keep you Eager
· Enough Friends to give you Comfort
· Enough Wealth to meet your Needs
· Enough enthusiasm to make you look Forward
· Enough Faith to banish depression, and
· Enough Determination to make each day a better
day than the last.

WHO I AM MAKES A DIFFERENCE

A teacher in a big city decided to honour each of her seniors in high school, by showing them that who they are made a difference. She called each student to the front of the class, one at a time. First she told each of them how they had made a difference to her and the class. Then she presented each of them with a blue ribbon imprinted with gold letters, which read, 'Who I Am Makes a Difference.'

Afterwards, the teacher decided to do a class project, to see what kind of impact recognition would have on a community. She gave each of the students three more ribbons and instructed them to go out and spread this acknowledgment ceremony. Then, they were to follow up on the results, see who honoured whom and report back to the class in about a week.

One of the boys in the class went to a junior executive in a nearby company and honoured him for helping him with his career planning. He gave him a blue ribbon and put it on his shirt. Then he gave him two extra ribbons and said, "We're doing a class project on recognition, and we'd like you to go out, find somebody to honour, give them a blue ribbon, then give them the extra blue ribbon so they can acknowledge a third person to keep this

39

acknowledgment ceremony going. Then please report back to me and tell me what happened."

Later that day, the junior executive went in to see his boss, who had been noted, by the way, as being kind of a grouchy fellow. He sat his boss down and he told him that he deeply admired him for being a creative genius.

The boss seemed very surprised. The junior executive asked him if he would accept the gift of the blue ribbon and would he give him permission to put it on him. His surprised boss said, "Well, sure." The junior executive took the blue ribbon and placed it right on his boss's jacket, above his heart.

As he gave him the last extra ribbon, he said, "Would you do me a favour? Would you take this extra ribbon and pass it on, by honouring somebody else? The young boy who first gave me the ribbons, is doing a project in school and he wants to keep this recognition ceremony going, to find out how it affects people."

That night, the boss came home to his 14-year-old son and sat him down. He said, "The most incredible thing happened to me today. I was in my office and one of the junior executives came in and told me he admired me and gave me a blue ribbon for being a creative genius. Imagine. He thinks I'm a creative genius. Then he put this blue ribbon that says, 'Who I Am Makes a Difference', on my jacket above my heart. He gave me an extra ribbon and asked me to find somebody else to honour. As I was driving home tonight, I started thinking about whom I would honour with this ribbon and I thought about you.

"I want to honour you. My days are really hectic and when I come home I don't pay a lot of attention to you. Sometimes I scream at you for not getting good enough grades in school and for your bedroom being a mess. But tonight, I just wanted to let you know that you do make a difference to me. Besides your mother, you are the most important person in my life. You're a great kid and I love you!"

The startled boy started to sob and sob, he couldn't stop crying. His whole body shook. He looked up at his father and said through his tears, "Dad, earlier tonight I sat in my room and wrote a letter to you and Mom, explaining why I had killed myself and asking you to forgive me. I was going to commit suicide tonight after you were asleep. I just didn't think that you cared at all. The letter is upstairs. I don't think I need it after all."

His father walked upstairs and found a heartfelt letter full of anguish and pain. The envelope was addressed, 'Mom and Dad.' The boss went back to work a changed man. He was no longer a grouch, but made sure to let all his employees know that they made a difference. The junior executive helped several other young people with career planning and never forgot to let them know that they made a difference in his life...one being the boss's son. And the young boy and his classmates learned a valuable lesson. Who you are *does* make difference.

You never know what kind of difference a little encouragement can make to a person.

HEAVEN'S VOICE MAIL?

Most of us have now learnt to live with voice mail as a necessary part of our lives. Have you ever wondered what it would be like if God decided to install voice mail? Imagine praying and hearing the following:

Thank you for calling heaven.

For English, press 1
For Spanish, press 2
For all other languages, press 3

Please select one of the following options:
Press 1 for requests
Press 2 for thanksgiving
Press 3 for complaints
Press 4 for all others

I am sorry. All our Angels and Saints are busy helping other sinners right now. However, your prayer is important to us and we will answer it in the order it was received. Please stay on the line.

If you would like to speak to:
God, press 1
Jesus, press 2
The Holy Spirit, press 3

To find a loved one that has been assigned to heaven, press 5, then enter his social security number, followed by the pound sign.

(If you receive a negative response, please hang up and dial area code 666)

For reservations to heaven, please enter JOHN followed by the numbers, 3 16.

For answers to nagging questions about dinosaurs, life and other planets, please wait until you arrive in heaven for the specifics.

Our computers show that you have already been prayed for today, please hang up and call again tomorrow.

The office is now closed for the weekend to observe a religious holiday.

If you are calling after hours and need emergency assistance, please contact your local pastor.

Thank you and have a heavenly day.

A LITTLE GIRL'S BROKEN PICTURE

Bruna Hoxholli arrived in Australia from Albania in 1995, to study at Avondale College. She graduated with a degree in education in 1998 then went on to do an honours degree [English] at Newcastle University, New South Wales.

The bus had followed the winding, snowy road for the past two hours. With my face against the frosty windows, my six-year-old imagination had already carried me to the house of the Snowman and back, at least four times.

The image outside the windows was stunning. Snow covered the ground, and high, rugged mountains formed a backdrop - their peaks played hide and seek with fluffy, grey clouds. A stream of cold water mirrored the barren trees (they had so much character, those trees).

We passed women wearing long, pleated skirts and woollen, flowery vests over flannelette shirts of a rainbow of colours. Men were dressed in their woollen trousers and pointed shoes. They wore little huts of white hats with a doggy tail of thread at the top.

We were travelling through the Northern Alps of Albania, an Alice's Wonderland, with white-covered magic, ancient tales and interesting people. Our home, for three days was the Seven Lakes, near the town of Kukës (close to the Albanian border with Kosovo).

For a six-year-old there was so much to do and many questions to ask: What bird is that? Why was the water warmish when it was snowing? What happened to the carrot nose of the snowman? Why is that old man beckoning me?

With the enthusiasm of a child discovering something new, everywhere she looked, I ran to him. He had one of those hats with the tail that I wanted so much to touch. He sat himself slowly on the snow, patted my hair, asked what my name was (it was a bit difficult to understand his strong Northern Albanian accent).

Then he took his hat off and put it on my head. Wow! I was actually wearing one of those things. I spent most of the day with this old man. His large, hard-worked hands were gentle with the snow, his voice soft, when telling ancient stories of Muji (a well-known myth in Northern Albania and Kosovo), the giant man who walked out of his grave, because he had given his word to fight against his village's enemy. Muji had given his word, and that was stronger than death for the Albanian.

Almost 20 years later and half a world away, it's 6:00pm. I watch television. I'm faced with worn, desperate faces, muddy shoes, crying children - refugees. For some, their only hope of survival is Kukës. But Kukës is different.

It's snowing, yes, but it is no longer Alice's Wonderland. Grey tents mar the magic whiteness of nature; sad faces have replaced the human expressions I remember.

As I watch, I catch my breath, and my eyes blink as if to avoid recognition. That old man, sitting tiredly on the soil, head on hand, tears on snow, hat on head – that's my old man of tender hands and soft voice.

I want to reach out through the screen and touch his broad shoulders. I yearn to tell him a nice story, to make him feel better.

Reality hits hard! He can't be my old man. If my old man were still alive, he'd be ancient now. And yet he is my old man. And that woman in the pleated skirt and woollen vest is my old woman. That man, that woman, that child - they are my people. And they're suffering in a realm of desperation that seems to know no human limits for misery.

And I want to cry out loud, because my framed mental picture has been torn to pieces and

47

trampled with muddy boots in sloppy snow. Why? Who's to blame?

Useless questions really. The issues are too complex to be resolved by empty accusations and hopeless answers. In fact, I refuse to ask these questions - not of God, not of fellow humans. I need my energy. The questions I allow myself to ask are, "Do they need me?" and "Can I help?" Yes, to both. I can pray. I can donate. So far, this is all I can do. Pointing fingers is time-consuming. Being angry with God or people is frustrating beyond consolation. Let's not do it!

Everyone needs to entertain rays of hope, no matter how dim their light. We need to help these people have some hope.

Bruna Hoxholli/Record/ANR 168
Used by permission

SPIRITUAL DEVELOPMENT?

Al Gore gave a big speech on 14 July 1999, about how his faith is so 'important' to him. In this attempt to convince the American people that we should consider him for president, he announced that his favourite Bible verse is John 16:3. Of course the speechwriter meant John 3:16, but nobody in the Gore camp was familiar enough with Scripture to catch the error.

Do you know what John 16:3 says? "And they will do this because they have not known the Father or me."

The Holy Spirit works in strange ways!

JESUS SAVES

Jesus and Satan were having an ongoing argument about who was better on the computer. They had been going at it for days and God was tired of hearing all the bickering.

Finally, God said, "Cool it. I am going to set up a test which will take two hours, and I will judge who does the better job."

So, Jesus and Satan sat down at the keyboards and typed away. They moused. They did spreadsheets. They wrote reports. They sent faxes. They sent e-mails. They sent e-mails with attachments. They downloaded. They did genealogy reports. They made cards. They did every known job.

But, ten minutes before the time was up, lightning suddenly flashed, thunder rolled, rain poured, and, of course, the electricity went off. Satan stared at his blank screen and screamed every curse word known in the underworld. Jesus just sighed.

The electricity finally came back on, and both of them started their computers. Satan started searching frantically, screaming, "It's gone! It's all gone! I lost everything when the power went out!"

Meanwhile, Jesus quietly started printing out all his files from the past two hours. Satan observed this and became more irate. "Wait! He cheated! How did he do it?!"
God shrugged and said, "Jesus Saves."

BUSY?

Satan called a worldwide convention of demons.

In his opening address he said, "We can't keep Christians from going to church. We can't keep them from reading their Bibles and knowing the truth. We can't even keep them from forming an intimate relationship with their Saviour. Once they gain that connection with Jesus, our power over them is broken.

"So let them go to their churches, but steal their time, so they don't have time to develop a relationship with Jesus Christ.

"This is what I want you to do", said the Devil. "Distract them from gaining hold of their Saviour and maintaining that vital connection throughout their day."

"How shall we do this?" his demons shouted.

"Keep them busy in the nonessentials of life and invent innumerable schemes to occupy their minds," he answered.

"Tempt them to spend, spend, spend, and borrow, borrow, borrow. Persuade their wives to go to work for long hours and their husbands to work 6-7 days each week, 10-12 hours a day, so they can afford their empty lifestyles.

"Keep them from spending time with their children. As their families fragment, soon their homes will offer no escape from the pressures of work! Over-stimulate their minds so that they cannot hear that still, small voice. Entice them to play the radio or cassette player whenever they drive.

"Keep the TV, VCR, CDs, DVD's and their PCs going constantly in their homes and see to it that every store and restaurant in the world plays non-biblical music constantly. This will jam their minds and break that union with their Christ.

"Fill the coffee tables with magazines and newspapers. Pound their minds with the news, 24 hours a day. Invade their driving moments with billboards. Flood their mailboxes with junk mail, mail order catalogues, sweepstakes, and every kind of newsletter and promotional offering free products, services and false hopes.

"Keep skinny, beautiful models on the magazines and TV, so their husbands will believe that outward beauty is what's important, and they'll become dissatisfied with their wives, and they will begin to look elsewhere.

"That will fragment their families quickly! "Give them Santa Claus, to distract them from teaching their children the real meaning of Christmas. Give them an Easter bunny, so they won't talk about his resurrection and power over sin and death. Even in their recreation, let them be excessive – have them return from their recreation exhausted. Keep them too busy to go out in nature and reflect on God's creation. Send them to amusement parks, sporting events, plays, concerts, and movies instead.

"Keep them busy, busy, busy!

"And when they meet for spiritual fellowship, involve them in gossip and small talk, so that they leave with troubled consciences.

"Crowd their lives with so many good causes they have no time to seek power from Jesus. Soon they will be working in their own strength, sacrificing their health and family for the good of the cause.

"It will work! It will work!"

It was quite a plan! The demons went eagerly to their assignments, causing Christians everywhere to get more busy and be more rushed, going here and there - having little time for their God or their families; having no time to tell others about the power of Jesus to change lives. I guess the question is, has the devil been successful at his scheme?

You be the judge!

What does busy mean for you?
B-eing **U**-nder **S**-atan's **Y**-oke?

RED WAGON

It was the day after Christmas at a church in San Francisco. The pastor of the church was looking over the cradle, when he noticed that the baby Jesus was missing from among the figures of the Nativity set.

He turned, went outside and saw a little boy with a red wagon, and in the wagon was the figure of the little infant, Jesus. He walked up to the boy and asked, "Well, where did you get him, my friend?" The little boy replied, "I got him from the church."
"And why did you take him?"
"Well, about a week before Christmas I prayed to the little Lord Jesus, and I told him that if he would bring me a red wagon for Christmas, I would give him a ride around the block in it."

THINGS ARE NOT ALWAYS WHAT THEY SEEM

Two travelling angels stopped to spend the night in the home of a wealthy family. The family was rude and refused to let the angels stay in their mansion's guestroom. Instead, the angels were given a small space in the cold basement. As they made their bed on the hard floor, the older angel saw a hole in the wall and repaired it. When the younger angel asked why, the older angel replied, "Things aren't always what they seem."

The next night, the pair came to rest at the house of a very poor, but very hospitable, farmer and his wife. After sharing what little food they had, the couple let the angels sleep in their bed, where they could have a good night's rest. When the sun came up the next morning, the angels found the farmer and his wife in tears. Their only cow, whose milk had been their sole income, lay dead in the field. The younger angel was infuriated and asked the older angel, "How could you have let this happen? The first man had everything, yet you helped him," he accused. "The second family had little but was willing to share everything, and you let their cow die."

"Things aren't always what they seem," the older angel replied. "When we stayed in the basement of the mansion, I noticed there was gold stored in that hole in the wall. Since the owner was so obsessed with greed and was unwilling to share his good fortune, I sealed the wall so that he wouldn't find it.

"Then, last night, as we slept in the farmer's bed, the angel of death came for his wife. I gave him the cow instead. Things aren't always what they seem."

Sometimes, that is exactly what happens when things don't turn out the way they should. If you have faith, you just need to trust that every outcome is always to your advantage. You might not know it, until some time later....

CHRISTMAS CAROLS

You may already know this, but I thought it interesting. There is one Christmas Carol that has always baffled me. What in the world do leaping lords, French hens, swimming swans, and especially the partridge who won't come out of the pear tree have to do with Christmas? Today I found out, thanks to the Internet. From 1558 through the next couple hundred years, the Church of England was the official religious centre, and Roman Catholics in England were not permitted to practice their faith openly. Someone during that era wrote this carol as a catechism song for young Catholics. It has two levels of meaning: the surface meaning plus a hidden meaning, known only to members of their church. Each element in the carol has a code word for a religious reality, which the children could remember:

The partridge in a pear tree was Jesus Christ.
Two turtle doves were the Old and New Testaments.
Three French hens stood for Faith, Hope and Love.
The four calling birds were the four gospels of Matthew, Mark, Luke & John.
The five golden rings recalled the Torah or Law, the first five books of the Old Testament.
The six geese a-laying stood for the six days of creation.

Seven swans a-swimming represented the sevenfold gifts of the Holy Spirit: Prophecy, Serving, Teaching, Exhortation, Contribution, Leadership, and Mercy.

The eight maids a-milking were the eight beatitudes.

Nine ladies dancing were the nine fruits of the Holy Spirit: Love, Joy, Peace, Patience, Kindness, Goodness, Faithfulness, Gentleness, and Self Control.

The ten lords a-leaping were the ten commandments.

The eleven pipers piping stood for the eleven faithful disciples.

The twelve drummers drumming symbolised the twelve points of belief in the Apostles' Creed.

So there is your history for today. This knowledge was shared with me and I found it interesting and enlightening about how that strange song became a Christmas Carol.

THE VISIT

Ruth went to her mailbox and found there was only one letter. She picked it up and looked at it before opening, but then she looked at the envelope again. There was no stamp, no postmark, only her name and address. She read the letter:

Dear Ruth,

I'm going to be in your neighbourhood on Saturday afternoon and I'd like to stop by for a visit.

Love Always,
Jesus

Her hands were shaking as she placed the letter on the table. "Why would the Lord want to visit me? I'm nobody special. I don't have anything to offer."

With that thought, Ruth remembered her empty kitchen cabinets. "Oh my goodness, I really don't have anything to offer. I'll have to run down to the store and buy something for dinner." She reached for her purse and counted out its contents. Five dollars and forty cents. "Well, I can get some bread and cold cuts, at least."

She threw on her coat and hurried out the door.

A loaf of French bread, a half-pound of sliced turkey, and a carton of milk...leaving Ruth with a grand total of twelve cents, to last her until Monday.

Nonetheless, she felt good as she headed home, her meagre offerings tucked under her arm.

"Hey lady, can you help us?"

Ruth had been so absorbed in her dinner plans, she hadn't even noticed two figures huddled in the alleyway. A man and a woman, both of them dressed in little more than rags.

"Look, I ain't got a job, ya know, and my wife and I have been living out here on the street, and, well, now it's getting cold and we're getting kinda hungry and, well, if you could help us, we'd really appreciate it."

Ruth looked at them both. They were dirty, they smelled bad and frankly, she was certain that they could get some kind of work if they really wanted to.

"Sir, I'd like to help you, but I'm a poor woman, myself. All I have is a few cold cuts and some bread, and I'm having an important guest for dinner tonight and I was planning on serving that to Him."

"Okay, I understand. Thanks anyway."

The man put his arm around the woman's shoulders, turned and headed back into the alley.

As she watched them leave, Ruth felt a familiar twinge in her heart.

"Sir, wait!" The couple stopped and turned as she ran down the alley after them. "Look, why don't you take this food. I'll figure out something else to serve my guest." She handed the man her grocery bag.

"Thank you, lady. Thank you very much!"
"Yes, thank you!" It was the man's wife, and Ruth could see that she was shivering. "You know, I've got another coat at home. Here, why don't you take this one." Ruth unbuttoned her jacket and slipped it over the woman's shoulders. Then, smiling, she turned and walked back to the street, without her coat and with nothing to serve her guest.

"Thank you, lady! Thank you very much!"

Ruth was chilled by the time she reached her front door, and worried too. The Lord was coming to visit and she didn't have anything to offer Him.

She fumbled through her purse for the door key.
But as she did, she noticed another envelope in her
mailbox.

"That's odd. The mailman doesn't usually come
twice in one day." She took the envelope out of the
box and opened it.

Dear Ruth,
It was so good to see you again. Thank you for the
lovely meal. And thank you, too, for the beautiful
coat.

Love Always
Jesus

The air was still cold, but even without her coat,
Ruth no longer noticed.

EMPTY EGGS

Jeremy was born with a twisted body and a slow mind. At the age of 12, he was still in second grade, seemingly unable to learn. His teacher, Doris Miller, often became exasperated with him.

He would squirm in his seat, drool and make grunting noises. At other times, he spoke clearly and distinctly, as if a spot of light had penetrated the darkness of his brain. Most of the time, however, Jeremy just irritated his teacher.

One day, she called his parents and asked them to come in for a consultation. As the Forresters entered the empty classroom, Doris said to them, "Jeremy really belongs in a special school. It isn't fair to him to be with younger children who don't have learning problems. Why, there is a five year gap between his age and that of the other students." Mrs. Forrester cried softly into a tissue, while her husband spoke. "Miss Miller," he said, "there is no school of that kind nearby. It would be a terrible shock for Jeremy if we had to take him out of this school. We know he really likes it here."

Doris sat for a long time after they had left, staring at the snow outside the window. Its coldness seemed to seep into her soul. She wanted to sympathise with the Forresters. After all, their only child had a terminal illness. But it wasn't fair to keep him in her class. She had 18 other youngsters to teach, and Jeremy was a distraction. Furthermore, he would never learn to read and write. Why waste any more time trying?

As she pondered the situation, guilt washed over her. *Here I am complaining when my problems are nothing compared to that poor family*, she thought. *Lord, please help me to be more patient with Jeremy.*

From that day on, she tried hard to ignore Jeremy's noises and his blank stares. Then one day, he limped to her desk, dragging his bad leg behind him. "I love you, Miss Miller," he exclaimed, loud enough for the whole class to hear. The other students snickered, and Doris' face turned red. She stammered, "Who…why that's very nice, Jeremy. N…now please take your seat."

Spring came, and the children talked excitedly about the coming of Easter. Doris told them the story of Jesus, and then to emphasise the idea of new life springing forth, she gave each of the children a large plastic egg.

"Now," she said to them, "I want you to take this home and bring it back tomorrow with something inside that shows new life. Do you understand?"

"Yes, Miss Miller," the children responded enthusiastically – all except for Jeremy. He listened intently; his eyes never left her face. He

64

didn't even make his usual noises. Had he understood what she had said about Jesus' death and resurrection? Did he understand the assignment? Perhaps she should call his parents and explain the project to them.

That evening, Doris' kitchen sink stopped up. She called the landlord and waited an hour for him to come by and unclog it. After that, she still had to shop for groceries, iron a blouse, and prepare a vocabulary test for the next day. She completely forgot about phoning Jeremy's parents.

The next morning, 19 children came to school, laughing and talking as they placed their eggs in the large wicker basket on Miss Miller's desk. After they completed their math lesson, it was time to open the eggs.

In the first egg, Doris found a flower. "Oh yes, a flower is certainly a sign of new life," she said. "When plants peek through the ground, we know that spring is here." A small girl in the first row waved her arm. "That's my egg, Miss Miller," she called out.

The next egg contained a plastic butterfly, which looked very real. Doris held it up. "We all know that a caterpillar changes and grows into a beautiful butterfly. Yes, that's new life, too." Little Judy smiled proudly and said, "Miss Miller, that one is mine."

Next, Doris found a rock with moss on it.
She explained that moss, too, showed life. Billy
spoke up from the back of the classroom, "My
daddy helped me," he beamed.

Then Doris opened the fourth egg. She gasped.
The egg was empty. Surely it must be Jeremy's she
thought, and of course, he did not understand the
instructions. If only she had not forgotten to phone
his parents. Because she did not want to embarrass
him, she quietly set the egg aside and reached for
another.

Suddenly, Jeremy spoke up. "Miss Miller, aren't
you going to talk about my egg?" Flustered, Doris
replied, "But, Jeremy, your egg is empty." He
looked into her eyes and said softly, "Yes, but
Jesus' tomb was empty, too." Time stopped.
When she could speak again, Doris asked him,
"Do you know why the tomb was empty?"
"Oh, yes," Jeremy said, "Jesus was killed and put
in there. Then His Father raised Him up."

The recess bell rang. While the children excitedly
ran out to the schoolyard, Doris cried. The
coldness inside her melted completely away.
Three months later, Jeremy died. Those who paid
their respects at the mortuary, were surprised to
see 19 eggs on top of his casket - all of them
empty.

NASA PROVES THAT GOD'S WORD IS TRUE

For all you scientists out there, here is something that gives evidence of God's awesome creation, and demonstrates that He is still in control.

Did you know that the space program is busy proving that, what has been called 'myth', in the Bible, is true?

Mr Harold Hill, President of the Curtis Engine Company in Baltimore, Maryland and a consultant in the space program, relate the following development:

"I think one of the most amazing things that God has for us today, happened recently to our astronauts and space scientists at Green Belt, Maryland. They were checking the position of the sun, moon, and planets out in space, and calculating where they would be 100 years and 1000 years from now. We have to know this information so that we don't send a satellite up and have it bump into something later on, during its orbits. We have to lay out the orbits in terms of the life of the satellite and where the planets will be, so the whole thing will not bog down. They ran the computer measurements back and forth over the centuries and it came to a halt.

"The computer stopped and put up a red signal, which meant that there was something wrong, either with the information fed into it or with the results as compared to the standards. They called in the service department to check it out. Well, they found there was a day missing in space, over the elapsed time. They scratched their heads and, figuratively, tore their hair out. They searched and searched for a solution. But, after many days, there was no answer to be found.

"Finally, a Christian man on the team said, "You know, one time I was in Sunday School and they talked about the sun standing still." While the others didn't believe him, they didn't have an answer either, so they said, "Show us." He got a Bible and went back to the book of Joshua, where they found a pretty ridiculous statement for any one with 'common sense'.

"There they found the Lord saying to Joshua, 'Fear them not, I have delivered them into thy hand; there shall not a man of them stand before thee.'

"Joshua was concerned because he was surrounded by the enemy but if darkness fell they could overpower them. So Joshua asked the Lord to make the sun stand still!

"That's right – 'The sun stood still and the moon stayed – and hasted not to go down about a whole day!' The astronauts and scientists said, "There is the missing day!"

"They checked the computers, going back into the time this text was written and found it was close, but not close enough. The elapsed time that was missing back in Joshua's day was 23 hours and 20 minutes – not a whole day. They read the Bible and there it was: "about (approximately) a day". These little words in the Bible are important, but they were still in trouble because if you cannot account for 40 minutes you'll still be in trouble 1,000 years from now. Forty minutes had to be found because it can be multiplied many times over in orbits.

As the Christian employee thought about it once again, he remembered somewhere in the Bible where it said the sun went backwards. The scientists told him he was out of his mind, but again they decided to check out the book and there they read these words in 2 Kings: Hezekiah, on his deathbed, was visited by the prophet Isaiah who told him that he was not going to die. Hezekiah asked for a sign as proof. Isaiah said, "Do you want the sun to go ahead 10 degrees?" Hezekiah said, "It is nothing for the sun to go ahead 10 degrees, but let the shadow return backward 10 degrees." Isaiah spoke to the Lord and the Lord brought the shadow ten degrees backward! Well, ten degrees is exactly 40 minutes! Twenty-three hours and 20 minutes in Joshua, plus 40 minutes in

2nd Kings make the missing day in the Universe! Isn't it amazing?

God and His Word is Truth!"

THE ANT, THE PRAYER, AND THE CONTACT LENS

Brenda was a young woman who was invited to go rock climbing. Although she was very scared, she went with her group to a tremendous granite cliff. In spite of her fear, she put on the gear, took a hold on the rope, and started up the face of that rock.

Well, she got to a ledge where she could take a breather. As she was hanging on there, the safety rope snapped against Brenda's eye and knocked out her contact lens.

So, there she was, on a rock ledge with hundreds of feet below her and hundreds of feet above her. Of course, she looked and looked, hoping it had landed on the ledge, but it just wasn't there.

Far from camp, her sight now blurry, she was desperate and began to get upset. So, she prayed to the Lord to help her to find it.

When she got to the top, a friend examined her eye and her clothing for the lens, but there was no contact lens to be found. She sat down, despondent, waiting for the rest of the party to make it up the face of the cliff.

She looked out across range after range of mountains, thinking of that verse that says,

'The eyes of the Lord run to and fro throughout the whole earth.' She thought, "Lord, You can see all these mountains. You know every stone and leaf, and You know exactly where my contact lens is. Please help me find it."

Finally, they walked down the trail to the bottom. At the bottom there was a new party of climbers just starting up the face of the cliff. One of them shouted out, "Hey, you guys! Anybody lose a contact lens?"

Well, that would be startling enough, but you know how the climber saw it? An ant was moving slowly across the face of the rock, carrying it on it's back.

Brenda told me that her father is a cartoonist. When she told him the incredible story of the ant, the prayer, and the contact lens, he drew a picture of an ant lugging that contact lens with the words, "Lord, I don't know why You want me to carry this thing. I can't eat it, and it's awfully heavy. But if this is what You want me to do, I'll carry it for You."

I think it would probably do some of us good to occasionally say, "God, I don't know why you want me to carry this load. I can see no good in it and it's awfully heavy. But, if you want me to carry it, I will."

God doesn't call the qualified, He qualifies the called. Yes, I do love God. He is my source of existence and my saviour. He keeps me functioning each and every day.

Without Him, I am nothing, but with Him...I can do all things, through Christ, who strengthens me.
Philippians 4:13

SWOLLEN BODY AND SHRIVELLED WINGS

One day, as a small opening appeared on a cocoon, a man sat for several hours watching the butterfly struggle to force its body through that little hole. Then, it seemed to stop making progress. It appeared as if it had gotten as far as it could and could go no further. So, the man decided to help the butterfly. He took a pair of scissors and snipped off the remaining bit of the cocoon. The butterfly then emerged easily, but it had a swollen body and small, shrivelled wings. The wings would enlarge and expand to be able to support the body, which would contract in time. But neither happened.

In fact, the butterfly spent the rest of its life crawling around with a swollen body and shrivelled wings. It never was able to fly. What the man, in his kindness and haste, did not understand was that the restricting cocoon and the struggle required for the butterfly to get through the tiny opening was nature's way of forcing fluid from the body of the butterfly into its wings. Then the butterfly would be ready for flight, once it achieved its freedom from the cocoon.

Sometimes struggles are exactly what we need in our life. If we were allowed to go through our life without any obstacles, it would cripple us.

We would not be as strong as we could be. We would never fly.

§

I asked for strength.
God gave me difficulties to make me strong.

I asked for wisdom.
God gave me problems to solve.

I asked for prosperity.
God gave me brain and brawn to work.

I asked for courage.
God gave me danger to overcome.

I asked for love.
God gave me troubled people to help.

I asked for favours.
God gave me opportunities.

I received nothing I wanted.
I received everything I needed.

SAYING GRACE

Last week, I took my children to a restaurant. My six-year-old son asked if he could say grace. As we bowed our heads, he said, "God is good. God is great. Thank you for the food, and I will thank you even more if Mom gets us ice cream for dessert. And liberty and justice for all! Amen!"

Along with the laughter from the other customers nearby, I heard a woman remark, "That's what's wrong with this country. Kids today don't even know how to pray. Asking God for ice-cream! Why, I never!"

Hearing this, my son burst into tears and asked me, "Did I do it wrong? Is God mad at me?" As I held him and assured him that he had done a terrific job and God was certainly not mad at him, an elderly gentleman approached the table. He winked at my son and said, "I happen to know that God thought that was a great prayer."
"Really?" my son asked.
"Cross my heart," the man replied.
Then, in a theatrical whisper, he added (indicating the woman whose remark had started this whole thing), "Too bad she never asks God for ice cream. A little ice cream is good for the soul sometimes."

Naturally, I bought my kids ice cream at the end of the meal. My son stared at his for a moment and then did something I will remember the rest of my life. He picked up his sundae and, without a word, walked over and placed it in front of the woman. With a big smile, he told her, "Here, this is for you. Ice cream is good for the soul sometimes; and my soul is good already."

INVISIBLE LOVE

The story goes that, some time ago, a man punished his 5-year-old daughter for wasting a roll of expensive gold wrapping paper. Money was tight and he became even more upset when the child pasted the gold paper, so as to decorate a box to put under the Christmas tree.

Nevertheless, the little girl brought the gift box to her father the next morning and said, "This is for you, Daddy." The father was embarrassed by his earlier over-reaction, but his anger flared again when he found that the box was empty. He spoke to her in a harsh manner, "Don't you know, young lady, when you give someone a present there's supposed to be something inside the package?" The little girl looked up at him with tears in her eyes and said, "Oh, Daddy, it's not empty. I blew kisses into it until it was full."

The father was crushed. He put his arms around his little girl and begged her to forgive him for his unnecessary anger.

An accident took the life of the child, only a short time later, and it is told that the father kept that gold box by his bed for all the years of his life. Whenever he was discouraged or faced difficult problems, he would open the box and take out an imaginary kiss and remember the love of the child who had put it there.

In a very real sense, each of us, as human beings, have been given a golden box filled with unconditional love and kisses from our children, family, friends and God. There is no more precious a possession anyone could hold.

LOVE STRANDED

Once upon a time, there was an island where all the feelings lived: Happiness, Sadness, Knowledge, and all the others, including Love.

One day, it was announced to all of the feelings that the island was going to sink to the bottom of the ocean. So, all the feelings prepared their boats to leave.

Love was the only one that stayed. She wanted to preserve the island paradise until the last possible moment.

When the island was almost totally under, Love decided it was time to leave.

She began looking for someone to ask for help. Just then, Richness was passing by in a grand boat. Love asked Richness, "Can I come with you in your boat?"

Richness answered, "I'm sorry, but there is a lot of silver and gold in my boat and there is no room for you anywhere."

Love decided to ask Vanity for help, who was passing in a beautiful vessel. Love cried out, "Vanity, help me please."

"I can't help you," Vanity said, "You are all wet and will damage my beautiful boat."

Next, Love saw Sadness passing by. "Sadness, please let me go with you," Love said. Sadness answered, "Love, I'm sorry, but, I just need to be alone now."

Then Love saw Happiness. Love cried out, "Happiness, please take me with you." But Happiness was so overjoyed that he didn't hear Love calling him.

Love began to cry. Then, she heard a voice say, "Come, Love, I will take you with me." It was an elder. Love felt so blessed and overjoyed that she forgot to ask the elder his name. When they arrived on land, the elder went on his way.

Love realised how much she owed the elder. She found Knowledge and asked, "Who was it that helped me?"
"It was Time," Knowledge answered.
"But why did Time help me when no one else would?" Love asked.

Knowledge smiled and with deep wisdom and sincerity, answered, "Because only Time is capable of understanding how great Love is."

WE ARE NEVER ALONE!

This is a true story that occurred in 1994, and is
told by Lloyd Glen:

Throughout our lives, we are blessed with spiritual
experiences, some of which are very sacred and
confidential, and others, although sacred, are
meant to be shared.

Last summer, my family had a spiritual experience
that had a lasting and profound impact on us - one
we feel must be shared. It is a message of love; a
message of regaining perspective, and restoring
proper balance and renewing priorities. In
humility, I pray that I might, in relating this story,
give you a gift, which my little son, Brian, gave
our family one summer day, last year.

On July 22nd, I was en-route to Washington DC for
a business trip. It was all so very ordinary, until we
landed in Denver for a plane change. As I collected
my belongings from the overhead bin, an
announcement was made for Mr. Lloyd Glenn to
see the United Customer Service representative
immediately.

I thought nothing of it, until I reached the door to
leave the plane and I heard a gentleman asking
every male if they were Mr Glenn. At this point I
knew something was wrong and my heart sunk.
When I got off the plane, a solemn-faced young

man came toward me and said, "Mr Glenn, there is an emergency at your home. I do not know what the emergency is, or who is involved, but I will take you to the phone so you can call the hospital."

My heart was now pounding, but the will to be calm took over. Woodenly, I followed this stranger to the distant telephone where I called the number he gave me for the Mission Hospital. My call was put through to the trauma centre where I learned that my three-year-old son had been trapped underneath the automatic garage door for several minutes, and that when my wife had found him he was dead. A neighbour, who is a doctor, had performed Cardio-Pulmonary Resuscitation and the paramedics had continued the treatment as Brian was transported to the hospital.

By the time of my call, Brian was revived and they believed he would live, but they did not know how much damage had been done to his brain, nor to his heart. They explained that the door had completely closed on his sternum, right over his heart. He had been severely crushed. After speaking with the medical staff, my wife sounded worried but not hysterical, and I took comfort in her calmness.

The return flight seemed to last forever, but finally, I arrived at the hospital, six hours after the garage door had come down. When I walked into the intensive care unit, nothing could have prepared

83

me to see my little son, lying so still on a great big bed with tubes and monitors everywhere. He was on a respirator. I glanced at my wife who stood and tried to give me a reassuring smile. It all seemed like a terrible dream. I was filled in with the details and given a guarded prognosis. Brian was going to live, and the preliminary tests indicated that his heart was okay, two miracles in and of themselves. But only time would tell if his brain had received any damage.

Throughout the seemingly endless hours, my wife was calm. She felt that Brian would eventually be all right. I hung onto her words and faith like a lifeline. All that night and the next day Brian remained unconscious. It seemed like forever since I had left for my business trip, the day before. Finally, at two o'clock that afternoon, our son regained consciousness and sat up uttering the most beautiful words I have ever heard spoken. He said, "Daddy, hold me." and he reached for me with his little arms.

By the next day, he was pronounced as having no neurological or physical deficits, and the story of his miraculous survival spread throughout the hospital. You cannot imagine our gratitude and joy. As we took Brian home, we felt a unique reverence for the life and love of our Heavenly Father that comes to those who brush with death so closely. In the days that followed, there was a special spirit about our home. Our two older children were much closer to their little brother. My wife and I were much closer to each other, and all of us were very close as a whole family. Life took on a less stressful pace. Perspective seemed to be more focused, and balance much easier to gain and maintain. We felt deeply blessed. Our gratitude was truly profound.

The story is not over!

Almost a month later, to the day of the accident, Brian awoke from his afternoon nap and said, "Sit down, mummy. I have something to tell you." At this time in his life, Brian usually spoke in small phrases; so to say a large sentence surprised my wife. She sat down with him on his bed and he began his remarkable story.

"Do you remember when I got stuck under the garage door? Well, it was so heavy and it hurt really bad. I called to you, but you couldn't hear me. I started to cry, but then it hurt too bad. And then the 'birdies' came."
 "The birdies?" my wife asked, puzzled.
 "Yes," he replied. "The birdies made a whooshing sound and flew into the garage. They took care of me."
"They did?"
"Yes" he said. "One of the birdies came and got you. She came to tell you I got stuck under the door." A sweet, reverent feeling filled the room. The spirit was so strong and yet lighter than air.

My wife realised that a three-year-old had no concept of death and spirits, so he was referring to the beings who came to him from beyond as 'birdies,' because they were up in the air like birds that fly.

"What did the birdies look like?" she asked. Brian answered, "They were so beautiful. They were dressed in white, all white. Some of them had green and white. But some of them had on just white."

"Did they say anything?"

"Yes," he answered. "They told me the baby would be alright."

"The baby?" my wife asked confused.

Brian answered. "The baby lying on the garage floor." He went on, "You came out and opened the garage door and ran to the baby. You told the baby to stay and not leave."

My wife nearly collapsed upon hearing this, for she had indeed gone and knelt beside Brian's body, and seeing his crushed chest and knowing he was already dead, she looked up around her and whispered, "Don't leave us Brian, please stay if you can." As she listened to Brian telling her the words she had spoken, she realised that the spirit had left his body.

"Then what happened?" she asked.

"We went on a trip." He said, "Far, far away." He grew agitated trying to say the things he didn't seem to have the words for. My wife tried to calm and comfort him, and let him know it would be okay. He struggled with wanting to tell something that obviously was very important to him, but finding the words was difficult.

"We flew so fast up in the air. They're so pretty Mummy," he added. "And there is lots and lots of birdies."

My wife was stunned. Into her mind the sweet comforting Spirit enveloped her more soundly, but with an urgency she had never known before. Brian went on to tell her that the 'birdies' had told him that he had to come back and tell everyone about the 'birdies'. He said they brought him back to the house and that a big fire truck, and an ambulance were there. A man was bringing the baby out on a white bed and he tried to tell the man that the baby would be okay, but the man couldn't hear him. He said the birdies told him he had to go with the ambulance, so they would be near him.

He said, they were so pretty and so peaceful, and he didn't want to come back.

Then the bright light came. He said that the light was so bright and so warm, and he loved the bright light so much. Someone was in the bright light and put their arms around him, and told him, "I love you. But you have to go back. You have to play baseball, and tell everyone about the birdies." Then the person in the bright light kissed him and waved bye-bye. Then whoosh, the big sound came and they went into the clouds.

The story went on for an hour. He taught us that 'birdies' are always with us, but we don't see them because we look with our eyes, and we don't hear them because we listen with our ears. But they are always there; you can only see them in here (he put his hand over his heart). They whisper things to help us to do what is right because they love us so much.

Brian continued, stating, "I have a plan, Mummy. You have a plan. Daddy has a plan. Everyone has a plan. We must all live our plan and keep our promises. The birdies help us to do that cause they love us so much."

In the weeks that followed, he often came to us and told all, or part of that story again and again. The story always remained the same. The details were never changed or out of order. A few times he added further bits of information and clarified the message he had already delivered. It never ceased to amaze us how he could tell such detail and speak beyond his ability, when he spoke of his 'birdies'. Everywhere he went, he told strangers about the 'birdies'. Surprisingly, no-one ever looked at him strangely when he did this. Rather, they always had a softened look on their face and smiled.

Needless to say, we have not been the same ever since that day, and I pray we never will be.

HEAVEN OR HELL?

"Well, Bill," said God, "I'm really confused on this one. I'm not sure whether to send you to Heaven or Hell. You made too many personal gains from society. Yet, you did contribute to the world by putting a computer in almost every home. I'm going to do something I've never done before: I'm going to let you decide where you want to go."

Mr. Gates replied, "Well, thanks, God. What's the difference between the two?"
God said, "You can take a peek at both places briefly, if it will help you decide. Shall we look at Hell first?"
"Sure." said Bill. "Let's go!"

Bill was amazed! He saw a clean, white sandy beach with clear waters. There were thousands of beautiful women running around, playing in the water, laughing and frolicking about. The sun was shining and the temperature was perfect!

Bill said, "This is great! If this is Hell, I can't wait to see Heaven!"
To which God replied, "Let's go!" and off they went.

Bill saw puffy white clouds in a beautiful blue sky, with angels drifting about playing harps and singing. It was nice, but surely not as enticing as

Hell. Mr. Gates thought for only a brief moment and rendered his decision.

"God, I do believe I would like to go to Hell."
"As you desire," said God.

Two weeks later, God decided to check up on the late billionaire, to see how things were going. He found Bill shackled to a wall, screaming among the hot flames, in a dark cave. He was being burned and tortured by demons.

"How ya doin', Bill?" asked God.
Bill responded with anguish and despair. "This is awful! This is not what I expected at all! What happened to the beach and the beautiful women playing in the water?"
"Oh, THAT!" said God. "That was the screen saver!"

WHERE WAS GOD ON SEPTEMBER 11?

Billy Graham's daughter was being interviewed on The Early Show.

Jane Clayson had asked her, "How could God let something like this happen?"

Anne Graham gave an extremely profound and insightful response.

She said, "I believe that God is deeply saddened by this, just as we are, but for years we've been telling God to get out of our schools, to get out of our government and to get out of our lives. And, being the gentleman that He is, I believe that He has calmly backed out.

"How can we expect God to give us His blessing and His protection if we demand that He leave us alone?

"Let's see, I think it started when Madeline Murray O'Hare (she was murdered, her body was found recently) complained she didn't want any prayer in our schools, and we said okay.

"Then someone said you better not read the Bible in school... the Bible that says thou shalt not kill, thou shalt not steal, and love your neighbour as yourself. And we said, okay.

"Then Dr. Benjamin Spock said we shouldn't spank our children when they misbehave, because their little personalities will be warped and we might damage their self-esteem (Dr. Spock's son committed suicide). And we said, an expert should know what he's talking about, so we said, okay.

"Then, someone said that teachers and principals better not discipline our children when they misbehave. And the school administrators said no faculty member in this school better touch a student when they misbehave because we don't want any bad publicity, and we surely don't want to be sued (There's a big difference between disciplining and touching, beating, smacking, humiliating, kicking, etc.) And we said, okay.

"Then someone said, let's let our daughters have abortions if they want, and they won't even have to tell their parents. And we said, okay.

"Then some wise school board member said, since boys will be boys and they're going to do it anyway, let's give our sons all the condoms they want, so they can have all the fun they desire, and we won't have to tell their parents they got them at school. And we said, okay.

"Then some of our top elected officials said it doesn't matter what we do in private, as long as we do our jobs. And agreeing with them, we said, "It doesn't matter to me what anyone, including the

President, does in private as long as I have a job and the economy is good."

"And then someone said let's print magazines with pictures of nude women and call it 'wholesome, down-to-earth appreciation for the beauty of the female body.' And we said, okay.

"And then someone else took that appreciation a step further and published pictures of nude children and then stepped further still, by making them available on the internet. And we said okay, they're entitled to their free speech.

"And then the entertainment industry said, let's make TV shows and movies that promote profanity, violence and illicit sex. And let's record music that encourages rape, drugs, murder, suicide, and satanic themes. And we said it's just entertainment, it has no adverse effect, and nobody takes it seriously anyway, so go right ahead.

"Now we're asking ourselves, why our children have no conscience? Why they don't know right from wrong? And why it doesn't bother them to kill strangers, their classmates and themselves?

"Probably, if we think about it long and hard enough, we can figure it out. I think it has a great deal to do with 'We reap what we sow'.

HELP ME TO FORGIVE

One day, a man was walking in the woods, his heart heavy with grief. As he thought about his life, he knew many things were not right.

He thought about those who had lied about him back when he had a job. His thoughts turned to those who had stolen his things and cheated him. He remembered family that had passed on. His mind turned to the illness he had that no one could cure.

His heart was filled with anger, resentment and frustration, as he stood there, searching for answers he could not find.

Knowing all else had failed him, he knelt at the base of an old oak tree to seek the One he knew would always be there. And with tears in his eyes, he prayed:
"Lord, You have done wonderful things for me in this life. You have told me to do many things for you, and I happily obeyed.

"Today, you told me to forgive. I am sad, Lord, because I can't. I don't know how to. It's not fair Lord. I didn't deserve these wrongs that were done against me and I shouldn't have to forgive. As perfect as your way is Lord, this one thing I cannot do, for I don't know how to forgive.

"My anger is so deep, Lord, I fear I may not hear you, but I pray that you will teach me to do this one thing I cannot do - teach me to forgive."

As he knelt there in the quiet shade of that old oak tree, he felt something fall onto his shoulder. He opened his eyes. Out of the corner of one eye, he saw something red on his shirt.

As he turned to see what it was, he saw that where the oak tree had been was a large square piece of wood in the ground. He raised his head and saw two feet held to the wood with a large spike through them. He raised his head more, and tears came to his eyes as he saw Jesus hanging on a cross. He saw spikes in His hands, a gash in His side, a torn and battered body, deep thorns sunk into His head. Finally, he saw the suffering and pain on His face.

As their eyes met, Jesus began to speak.
"Have you ever told a lie?" he asked.
The man answered, "Yes, Lord."
"Have you ever been given too much change and kept it?"
The man answered, "Yes, Lord." "Have you ever taken something from work that wasn't yours?" Jesus asked.
And the man answered, "Yes, Lord."
"Have you ever sworn, using my Father's name in vain?"
The man, crying now, answered, "Yes, Lord!"

As Jesus asked many more times, "Have you ever…?"
The man's crying became uncontrollable, for he could only answer, "Yes, Lord."

Then, Jesus turned His head from one side to the other, and the man felt something fall on his other shoulder. He looked and saw that it was the blood of Jesus.

When he looked back up, his eyes met those of Jesus, and there was a look of love the man had never seen or known before. Jesus said, "I didn't deserve this either, but I forgive you."

It may be hard to see how you're going to get through something, but when you look back in life, you realise how true this statement is: *If God brings you to it, He will bring you through it.*

Lord, I love You and I need You. Come into my heart today. For without You, I can do nothing that is good.

TALKING WITH GOD

Once I dreamt I had an interview with God.

"So, you would like to interview me?" God asked.

"If you have the time," I said.

God said with a smile, "My time is eternity. What questions would you like to ask me?"

"What surprises you most about mankind?"

God answered, "That they get bored with childhood. They rush to grow up, and then long to be children again.

"That they lose their health to make money, and then lose their money to restore their health.

"That, by thinking anxiously about the future, they forget the present, in such a way that they live in neither the present, nor the future.

"That they live as if they will never die, and die as if they had never lived."

God's hand took mine, and we were silent for a while. Then I asked, "As a parent, what are some of life's lessons you want your children to learn?"

God replied with a smile, "To learn they cannot make anyone love them. What they can do is let themselves be loved.

"To learn that it is not good to compare themselves to others.

"To learn that a rich person is not one who has the most, but is one who needs the least.

"To learn that it only takes a few seconds to make deep wounds in the people we love, but it takes many years to heal them.

"To learn to forgive by practising forgiveness.

"To learn that there are people who love them dearly, but simply do not know how to express or show their feelings.

"To learn that two people can look at the same thing and see it differently.

"To learn that it is not always enough that they be forgiven by others, but that they must forgive themselves.

"And to learn that I am always here."

UNCONDITIONAL ACCEPTANCE

Here is a great story that we all can learn something from....

I am a mother of three (ages 14, 12, 3) and have recently completed my college degree.

The last class I had to take was Sociology. The teacher was really inspiring, with the qualities that I wish every human being had been graced with.

Her last project of the term was called 'Smile.' The class was asked to go out and smile at three people and document their reactions. I am a very friendly person and always smile at everyone and say hello anyway. So I thought this would be a piece of cake.

Soon after we were assigned the project, my husband, youngest son and I went out to McDonald's, on a crisp March morning. It was just our way of sharing special playtime with our son. We were standing in line, waiting to be served, when all of a sudden everyone around us began to back away, and then even my husband did.

I didn't move an inch, but an overwhelming feeling of panic welled up inside of me, as I turned to see why they had moved. As I turned around, I noticed a horrible 'dirty body' smell, and there, standing behind me, were two homeless men.

As I looked down at the short gentleman, close to me, I noticed that he was smiling. His beautiful sky blue eyes were full of God's Light, as he searched for acceptance. He said, "Good day" as he counted the few coins he had been clutching. The second man fumbled with his hands as he stood behind his friend. I realised the second man was mentally challenged and the blue-eyed gentleman was his saviour.

I held my tears as I stood there with them. The young lady at the counter asked him what they wanted. "Coffee is all, Miss," he said, because that was all they could afford. If they wanted to sit in the restaurant and warm up, they had to buy something.

Then, I felt a compulsion so great that I almost reached out and embraced the little man with the blue eyes. That is when I noticed all eyes in the restaurant were set on me, as if they were judging my every action.

I smiled and asked the young lady behind the counter to give me two more breakfast meals on a tray. I then walked around the corner to the table that the men had chosen as a resting spot. I put the tray on the table and laid my hand on the blue-eyed gentleman's cold hand. He looked up at me, with tears in his eyes, and said, "Thank you." I leaned over, began to pat his hand and said, "I did not do this for you. God is here working through me to give you hope."

I started to cry as I walked away to join my husband and son. When I sat down my husband smiled at me and said, "That is why God gave you to me, Honey. To give me hope."

That day showed me the pure light of God's sweet love.

I returned to college on the last evening of class, with this story in hand. I turned in my project and the instructor read it. Then, she looked up at me and asked, "Can I share this?" I nodded.

We, as human beings, and being children of God, share a need to heal people and to be healed. In my own way, I touched the people at McDonald's, my husband, son, instructor, and every soul that I shared that classroom with on the last night I spent as a college student. I graduated with one of the biggest lessons I would ever learn: *Unconditional Acceptance.*

GIDEON'S TWENTY

One Sunday morning, during the service, a 2000-member congregation was surprised to see two men enter, both covered from head to toe in black and carrying sub-machine guns. One of the men proclaimed, "Anyone willing to take a bullet for Christ remain where you are."

Immediately, the choir fled, the deacons fled and most of the congregation fled. Out of the 2000 only 20 stayed.

The man who had spoken took off his hood, looked at the preacher and said "Okay Pastor, I got rid of all the hypocrites. You can now continue your service. Have a nice day!"

And the two men turned and walked out.

(Note: The church, however, is a hospital, so keep on attending. Ed.)

THE ATHEIST AND THE BEAR

As an atheist was walking through the forest, he smiled at the beauty that was all around him and said, "What natural wonders the powers of evolution have created." Just then, he heard a rustling near the river and he went to investigate. He saw a seven-foot-tall grizzly bear was tearing down the path towards him.

The man took off like a shot, and when he got the courage to look back, he saw the bear was catching up fast. He tried with all his strength to pick up the pace, but he tripped and crashed to the ground. As he tried to get up, the bear jumped on him and picked up a paw to whack him. "Oh my God!!!" the atheist screamed.

Time stopped. The bear froze. The forest was silent. Even the river stopped moving. A bright light shone upon the man and a voice boomed from the heavens, "You have denied my existence for all of these years. You teach others that I don't exist, and even credit Creation to a cosmic accident. Do you expect me to help you out of this predicament? Am I to count you as a believer?"

The atheist looked directly into the light, "It would be hypocritical of me to suddenly ask you to treat me as a Christian now, but perhaps you could make the bear a Christian?"

"Very well," the voice said.

The light went out, the river ran again, and the sounds of the forest resumed. And then the bear dropped its raised paw, brought both of then together, bowed its head and spoke: "Lord, for this food that I am about to receive, I am truly thankful."

EVOLUTION EXPLAINED

One day, a 6-year-old girl was sitting in a classroom. The teacher was trying to explain evolution to the children.

Teacher: Tommy, do you see the tree outside?
Tommy: Yes.

Teacher: Can you see the grass outside?
Tommy: Yes.

Teacher: Go outside and look up and see if you can see the sky.
Tommy: Okay. (He returned a few minutes later) Yes, I saw the sky.

Teacher: Did you see God?
Tommy: No.

Teacher: That's my point. We can't see God because he isn't there. He doesn't exist.

The little girl spoke up, wanting to ask the boy some questions. The teacher agreed and the little girl asked the boy:

Little Girl: Tommy, do you see the tree outside?
Tommy: Yes.

Little Girl: Can you see the grass outside?
Tommy: Yessssss (getting tired of the questions by this time).

Little Girl: Did you see the sky?
Tommy: Yessssss

Little Girl: Tommy, do you see the teacher?
Tommy: Yes

Little Girl: Do you see her brain?
Tommy: No

Little Girl: Then according to what we were taught today, she must not have one!

For we walk by faith, not by sight.

LUNCH WITH GOD

There was once a boy who wanted to meet God.
He knew it was a long trip to where God lived, so
he packed his backpack with cookies and a six-
pack of root beer, and started on his journey.

When he had gone about three blocks, he met an
old woman. She was sitting in the park just staring
at some pigeons. The boy sat down next to her and
opened his backpack. He was about to take out a
drink of root beer when he noticed that the old lady
looked hungry, so he offered her a cookie. She
gratefully accepted it and smiled at him. Her smile
was so pretty that the boy wanted to see it again, so
he offered her a root beer. Again, she smiled at
him. The boy was delighted!

They sat there all afternoon, eating and smiling,
but neither said a word. As it grew dark, the boy
realised how tired he was and he got up to leave.
But, before he had gone more than a few steps, he
turned around, ran back to the old woman and gave
her a hug. She gave him her biggest smile ever.

When the boy opened the door to his own house a
short time later, his mother was surprised by the
look of joy on his face. She asked him, "What did
you do today that made you so happy?"
He replied, "I had lunch with God." And before his
mother could respond, he added, "You know

what? She has the most beautiful smile I've ever seen!"

Meanwhile, the old woman, also radiant with joy, returned to her home. Her son was stunned by the look of peace on her face and asked, "Mother, what did you do today that made you so happy?" She replied, "I ate cookies in the park with God." And before her son could respond, she added, "You know, he's much younger than I expected."

Too often we underestimate the power of a touch, a smile, a kind word, a listening ear, an honest compliment, or the smallest act of care; all of which have the potential to turn a life around. Remember, we don't know what God will look like. People come into our lives for a reason, a season, or a lifetime.

THE CENTRE OF THE BIBLE

This is pretty strange or odd that it worked out this way.

Q. What is the shortest chapter in the Bible?

A. Psalms 117

Q. What is the longest chapter in the Bible?

A. Psalms 119

Q. Which chapter is in the centre of the Bible?

A. Psalms 118

Fact: There are 594 chapters *before* Psalms 118 and 594 chapters *after* Psalms 118.

Add these numbers up and you get 1188.

Q. What is the centre verse in the Bible?

A. Psalms 118:8

Does this verse say something significant about God's perfect will for our lives?

Psalms 118:8 (NKJV) – "It is better to trust in the Lord than to put confidence in man."

The next time someone says they would like to find God's perfect will for their lives and that they want to be in the centre of His will, just send them to the centre of His Word!

Now isn't that odd how this worked out (or was God in the centre of it)?

A HELPING HAND

One day, when I was a freshman in high school, I saw a kid from my class walking home from school. His name was Kyle. It looked as though he was carrying all of his books. I thought to myself, *Why would anyone bring home all his books on a Friday? He must really be a nerd.* I had quite a weekend planned (parties and a football game with my friends the next afternoon), so I shrugged my shoulders and went on.

As I was walking, I saw a bunch of kids running toward him. They ran at him, knocking all his books out of his arm. As he crawled around looking for his glasses, I saw a tear in his eye. I handed him his glasses and said, "Those guys are jerks. They really should get lives." He looked at me and said, "Hey, thanks!" There was a big smile on his face. It was one of those smiles that showed real gratitude.

I helped him pick up his books and asked him where he lived.

As it turned out, he lived near me, so I asked why I had never seen him before. He said he had gone to a private school. I would have never hung out with a private school kid before. We talked all the way home, and I carried some of his books. He turned out to be a pretty cool kid. I asked him if he

111

wanted to play some football with my friends. He said yes. So, we ended up hanging out all weekend, and the more I got to know Kyle, the more I liked him, and my friends thought the same of him.

Monday morning came, and there was Kyle with the huge stack of books again. I stopped him and said, "Boy, you are gonna build some serious muscles with this pile of books everyday!" He just laughed and handed me half.

Over the next four years, Kyle and I became best friends. When we were seniors, we began to think about college. Kyle decided on Georgetown, and I was going to Duke. I knew that we would always be friends; that the miles would never be a problem. He was going to be a doctor, and I was going for business on a football scholarship.

Kyle was valedictorian of our class. I teased him all the time about being a nerd. He had to prepare a speech for graduation. But, I was so glad it wasn't me having to get up there and speak.

Graduation day came and Kyle looked great. He was one of those guys that really found himself during high school. I could see that he was nervous about his speech, so I smacked him on the back and said, "Hey, big guy, you'll be great!" He looked at me with one of those looks (the really grateful one) and smiled. "Thanks", he said.

As he took the place at the podium, he cleared his throat, and began.

"Graduation is a time to thank those who helped you make it through those tough years. Your parents, your teachers, your siblings, maybe a coach...,but mostly, your friends. I am here to tell all of you that being a friend to someone is the best gift you can give them. I'm going to tell you a story."

I looked at my friend with disbelief as he told the story of the first day we met. He had planned to kill himself over the weekend. He talked of how he had cleaned out his locker so that his Mom wouldn't have to do it later, and was carrying his stuff home. He looked hard at me and gave me a little smile. "Thankfully, I was saved. My friend saved me from doing the unspeakable." I heard the gasp go through the crowd as this handsome, popular boy told us all about his weakest moment. I saw his Mom and Dad looking at me and smiling that same grateful smile. Not until that moment did I realise its depth.

God puts us all in each other's lives to impact one another in some way. Never underestimate the power of your actions. With one small gesture you can change a person's life. For better or for worse.

THE KEY TO TRUE HAPPINESS

One day, a friend asked another, "How is it that you are always so happy? You have so much energy, and you never seem to get down."
"With her eyes smiling, she said, "I know the secret!"
"What secret is that?"
"I'll tell you all about it, but you have to promise to share the secret with others.

"The secret is this: I have learned there is little I can do in my life that will make me truly happy. I must depend on God to make me happy and to meet my needs. When a need arises in my life, I have to trust God to supply, according to His riches. I have learned that most of the time I don't need half of what I think I do. He has never let me down. Since I learned that secret, I've been happy."

The questioner's first thought was, *'That's too simple!'* But upon reflecting over her own life, she recalled how she thought a bigger house would make her happy, but it didn't. She thought a better paying job would make her happy, but it hadn't. When did she realise her greatest happiness? Sitting on the floor with her grandchildren, playing games, eating pizza or reading a story.

Now you know it too! We can't depend on people to make us happy. Only God in His infinite wisdom can do that. Trust Him!

P.U.S.H.

One night, a man was sleeping in his cabin when suddenly, his room filled with light and the Saviour appeared. The Lord told the man he had work for him to do, and showed him a large rock in front of his cabin.

The Lord explained that the man was to push against the rock with all his might. This the man did, day after day.

For many years, he toiled from sunrise to sundown, his shoulders set squarely against the cold, massive surface of the unmoving rock, pushing with all his might. Each night, the man returned to his cabin, sore and worn out, feeling that his whole day had been spent pushing in vain.

Since the man was showing signs of discouragement, an adversary decided to enter the picture, by placing discouraging thoughts in his mind: *You have been pushing against that rock for a long time, and it hasn't budged. Why kill yourself over this? You are never going to move it.* Thus, the man got the impression that the task was impossible and that he was a failure.

These thoughts discouraged and disheartened the man. *Why kill myself over this?* he thought. *I'll just put in my time, giving the minimum effort. That will be good enough.*

And that is what he planned to do. Until, one day, he decided to make it a matter of prayer and take his troubled thoughts to the Lord.

"I have laboured long and hard in your service, putting all my strength to do that which you have asked. Yet, after all this time, I have not even budged that rock by half a millimetre. What is wrong? Why am I failing?"

The Lord responded compassionately, "My friend, when I asked you to serve me and you accepted, I told you that your task was to push against the rock with all your strength, which you have done. Never once did I mention to you that I expected you to move it. Your task was to push. And now you come to me with your strength spent, thinking that you have failed.

"But is that really so? Look at yourself. Your arms are strong and muscled; your back is sinewy and strong; your hands are callused from constant pressure; and your legs have become massive and hard. Through opposition you have grown much, and your abilities now surpass those which you used to have. Yet, you haven't moved the rock.

Your calling was to be obedient, to push and to exercise your faith and trust in My wisdom.

This you have done. I, my friend, will now move the rock."

At times, when we hear a word from God, we tend to use our own intellect to decipher what He wants. When what God actually wants is just obedience and faith in Him. By all means exercise the faith that moves mountains, but know that it is still God who moves the mountains.

When everything seems to go wrong ... just PUSH!

When your job gets you down ... just PUSH!

When people don't react the way you think they should ... just PUSH!

When people just don't understand you ... just PUSH!

PUSH ... **P**ray **U**ntil **S**omething **H**appens!

HIDDEN BLESSINGS

A water bearer in India had two large pots, each hung on the ends of a pole, which he carried across his neck.

One of the pots had a crack in it, while the other pot was perfect and always delivered a full portion of water. At the end of the long walk from the stream to the house, the cracked pot arrived only half full.

For a full two years this went on daily, with the bearer delivering only one and a half pots full of water to his house. Of course, the perfect pot was proud of its accomplishments, perfect for which it was made. But the poor cracked pot was ashamed of its own imperfection, and miserable that it was able to accomplish only half of what it had been made to do.

After 2 years of what it perceived to be bitter failure, it spoke to the water bearer one day, by the stream. "I am ashamed of myself, and I want to apologise to you. I have been able to deliver only half my load because this crack in my side causes water to leak out all the way back to your house. Because of my flaws, you have to do all of this work, and you don't get full value from your efforts," the pot said.

The bearer said to the pot, "Did you notice that there were flowers only on your side of the path, but not on the other pot's side? That's because I have always known about your flaw, and I planted flower seeds on your side of the path, and every day while we walk back, you've watered them. For two years I have been able to pick these beautiful flowers to decorate the table. Without you being just the way you are, there would not be this beauty to grace the house."

Moral: Each of us has our own unique flaws. We're all cracked pots. But it's the cracks and flaws we each have that make our lives together so very interesting and rewarding. You've just got to take each person for what they are, and look for the good in them.

Remember to appreciate all the different people in your life!

Blessed are the flexible, for they shall not be bent out of shape.

KEEP YOUR FORK

The world crowns success
God crowns faithfulness.

There was once a woman who had been diagnosed
with a terminal illness and had been given three
months to live.

As she was getting her things *in order* she
contacted her pastor and had him come to her
house to discuss certain aspects of her final wishes.
She told him which songs she wanted sung at the
service, what scripture she would like read and
what outfit she wanted to be buried in. The woman
also requested to be buried with her favourite
Bible.

Everything was in order and the pastor was
preparing to leave when the woman suddenly
remembered something very important to her.
"There's one more thing," she said excitedly.
"What's that?" came the pastor's reply.
"This is very important," the woman continued. "I
want to be buried with a fork in my right hand."

The pastor stood looking at the woman, not
knowing quite what to say.
"That surprises you, doesn't it?" the woman asked.
"Well, to be honest, I'm puzzled by the request,"
said the pastor.

The woman explained. "In all my years of attending church socials and potluck dinners, I always remember that when the dishes of the main course were being cleared, someone would inevitably lean over and say, 'Keep your fork.' It was my favourite part, because I knew that something better was coming . . . like velvety chocolate cake or deep-dish apple pie. Something wonderful and with substance! So, I just want people to see me in that casket with a fork in my hand and I want them to wonder, 'What's with the fork?' Then I want you to tell them: 'Keep your fork. . .the best is yet to come.'"

The pastor's eyes welled up with tears of joy as he hugged the woman goodbye. He knew this would be one of the last times he would see her before her death. But, he also knew that the woman had a better grasp of heaven than he did. She knew, without a doubt, that something better was coming.

At the funeral, people were walking by the woman's casket and they saw the pretty dress she was wearing and her favourite Bible and the fork placed in her right hand. Over and over, the pastor heard the question, "What's with the fork?" And over and over he smiled.

During his message, the pastor told the people of the conversation he had with the woman, shortly before she died. He also told them about the fork and about what it symbolised to her. The pastor told the people how he could not stop thinking about the fork and told them that they probably would not be able to stop thinking about it either.

He was right!

So the next time you reach down for your fork, let it remind you, oh so gently, that the best is yet to come!

"Faith is the assurance of things hoped for, the conviction of things not seen."
- Hebrews 11:1

YOUR CROSS

A young man was at the end of his rope. Seeing no way out, he dropped to his knees in prayer:

"Lord, I can't go on," he said. "I have too heavy a cross to bear."

The Lord replied, "My son, if you can't bear its weight, just place your cross inside this room. Then, open that other door and pick out any cross you wish."

The man was filled with relief. "Thank you Lord," he said, and did as he was told.

Upon entering the other room, he saw many crosses; some so large that the tops were not visible. Then, he spotted a tiny cross, leaning against a far wall.

"I'd like that one, Lord," he whispered.

The Lord replied, "My son, that is the cross you just brought in."

When life's problems seem overwhelming, it helps to look around and see what other people are coping with. You may consider yourself far more fortunate than you had imagined.

§

Whatever your cross
Whatever your pain
There will always be sunshine
After the rain.

Perhaps you may stumble
Perhaps even fall
But God's always there
To help you through it all.

PRAYERS

THE LORD'S PRAYER

'Our Father which art in heaven,'

    --- Yes?

Don't interrupt me. I'm praying.

    --- But you called me.

Called you? I didn't call you. I'm praying. 'Our Father which art in heaven,'

    --- There you did it again.

Did what?

    --- Called me. You said, 'Our Father which art in heaven.' Here I am. What's on your mind?

But I didn't mean anything by it. I was, you know, just saying my prayers for the day. I always say the Lord's Prayer. It makes me feel good, kind of like getting a duty done.

    --- All right. Go on.

'Hallowed be Thy name.'

    --- Hold it. What do you mean by that?

By what?

     --- By 'Hallowed be Thy name?'

It means. It means.... Good grief, I don't know
what it means. How should I know? It's just a part
of the prayer. By the way, what does it mean?

     --- It means honoured, holy, wonderful.

Hey, that makes sense. I never thought about what
'hallowed' meant before. 'Thy kingdom come,
Thy will be done, on earth as it is in heaven.'

     --- Do you really mean that?

Sure, why not?

     --- What are you doing about it?

Doing? Nothing, I guess. I just think it would be
kind of neat if you got control of everything down
here, like you have up there.

     --- Have I got control of you?

Well, I go to church.

     --- That isn't what I asked you. What about
     your temper? You've really got a problem
     there, you know. And then there's the way
     you spend your money all on yourself. And

what about the kinds of books you read and
what you watch on TV?

Stop picking on me! I'm just as good as the rest of
those people at church.

      ---Excuse me! I thought you were praying
for My will to be done. If that is to happen,
it will have to start with the ones who are
praying for it. Like you, for example.

Oh, all right. I guess I do have some hang-ups.
Now that you mention it, I could probably name
some others.

      ---So could I.

I haven't thought about it very much until now, but
I'd really like to cut out some of those things. I
would like to, you know, be really free.

      --- Good. Now we're getting somewhere.
We'll work together, you and I. Some
victories can be truly won. I'm proud of
you.

Look, Lord, I need to finish this up, here. This is
taking a lot longer than it usually does...'Give us
this day our daily bread.'

      --- You could cut out the bread. It would
help you lose weight.

Hey, wait a minute! What is this, 'Criticize Me Day?' Here I was doing my religious duty, and all of a sudden you break in and remind me of all my hang-ups.

> --- Praying is a dangerous thing. You could end up changed, you know. That's what I'm trying to get across to you. Keep praying. I'm interested in the next part of your prayer.

(Pause)

> --- Well, go on.

I'm scared to.

> --- Scared? Of what?

I know what you'll say.

> --- Try me and see.

Forgive us our sins, as we forgive those who sin against us.

> --- What about Ann?

See? I knew it! I knew you would bring her up! Why, Lord, she's told lies about me, spread stories about my family. And she never paid back the money she owes me. I've sworn to get even with her!

> --- But your prayer? What about your prayer?

I didn't mean it.

> --- Well, at least you're honest. But it's not much fun carrying that load of bitterness inside you, is it?

No. But, I'll feel better as soon as I get even. Boy, have I got some plans for that neighbour. She'll wish she had never moved into this neighbourhood.

> ---You won't feel any better. You'll feel worse. Revenge isn't sweet. Think of how unhappy you already are. But, I can change all that.

You can? How?

> --- Forgive Ann. Then I'll forgive you. Then the hate and sin will be Ann's problem and not yours. You will have settled your heart.

Oh, you're right. You always are. And, more than I want to get revenge against Ann, I want to be right with you. But ... (Pause)...(Sigh) ... All right. I forgive her. Help her to find the right road in life, Lord. She's bound to be awfully miserable, now that I think about it. Anybody who goes around doing the things she does to others has to be out of it. Someway, somehow, show her the right way.

--- There now! Wonderful! How do you feel?

Hmmm. Well, not bad. Not bad at all. I feel pretty great. You know, I don't think I'll be going to bed feeling uptight tonight, for the first time since I can remember. Maybe I won't be so tired from now on, because I'm not getting enough rest.

--- You're not through with your prayers. Go on.

Oh, all right. 'And lead us not into temptation, but deliver us from evil.'

--- Good! Good! I'll do that. Just don't put yourself in a place where you can be tempted.

What do you mean by that?

--- Don't turn the TV on when you know the laundry needs to be done and the house needs to be tidied up. Also, about the time you spend with your friends, if you can't influence the conversation to positive

132

things, perhaps you should rethink the value of those friendships. Another thing, your neighbours and friends shouldn't be your standard for 'keeping up'. And please don't use me as an escape hatch.

I don't understand that last part.

--- Sure you do. You've done it a lot of times. You get caught in a bad situation. You get in trouble and then you come running to me: "Lord, help me out of this mess, and I promise you I'll never do it again." You remember some of those bargains you tried to make with me?

Yes, and I'm ashamed, Lord, I really am.

---Which bargain are you remembering?

Well, there was the night that my husband was gone and the children and I were home alone. The wind was blowing so hard I thought the roof would go any minute and tornado warnings were out. I remember saying, "Oh God, if you spare us, I'll never skip my devotions again."

--- I protected you, but you didn't keep your promise, did you?
I'm sorry, Lord, I really am. Up until now I thought that if I just prayed the Lord's Prayer

every day, then I could do what I liked. I didn't expect anything to happen like this.

--- Go ahead and finish your prayer.

'For Thine is the kingdom, and the power, and the glory, forever. Amen.'

--- Do you know what would bring me glory? What would really make me happy?

No, but I'd like to know. I want to please you. I can see what a mess I've made of my life. And I can see how great it would be to really be one of your followers.

--- You just answered the question.

I did?

--- Yes. The thing that would bring me glory is to have people like you, truly love me. And I see that happening between us. Now that some of these old sins are exposed and out of the way, there is no telling what we can do together.

Lord, let's see what we can make of me, okay?

--- Yes, let's see.

DON'T REPEAT THE LORD'S PRAYER. PRAY IT.

A PRAYER AT SENATE OPENING

When Minister Joe Wright was asked to open the new session of the Kansas State Senate, everyone was expecting the usual generalities, but this is what they got:

"Heavenly Father, we come before you today to ask your forgiveness and to seek your direction and guidance. We know Your Word says, "Woe to those who call evil good", but that is exactly what we have done. We have lost our spiritual equilibrium and reversed our values. We confess that.

"We have ridiculed the absolute truth of Your Word and called it Pluralism.
We have exploited the poor and called it the Lottery.
We have rewarded laziness and called it welfare.
We have killed our unborn and called it choice.
We have shot abortionists and called it justifiable.
We have neglected to discipline our children and called it building self-esteem.
We have abused power and called it politics.
We have coveted our neighbours' possessions and called it ambition.
We have polluted the air with profanity and pornography and called it freedom of speech.

135

We have ridiculed the time-honoured values of our forefathers and called it enlightenment.

"Search us, Oh God, and know our hearts today. Cleanse us from every sin and set us free. Guide and bless these men and women who have been sent to direct us to the centre of Your will and to openly ask these things, in the name of Your Son, the living Saviour, Jesus Christ, Amen."

§

The response was immediate. A number of legislators walked out during the prayer in protest. In a few weeks, the Central Christian Church, where Rev. Wright is pastor, logged more than 5,000 calls with only 47 of those calls responding negatively. The church is now receiving international requests for copies of this prayer from India, Africa and Korea. Commentator Paul Harvey aired this prayer on his radio program, 'The Rest of the Story', and received a larger response to this programme than any other he has ever aired.

With the Lord's help, may this prayer sweep over our nation and wholeheartedly become our desire, so that we, again, can be called, 'one nation under God.'

POWER OF PRAYER

Prayer is one of the best free gifts we receive.
There is no cost but a lot of rewards.

§

May there be peace within you today.
May you trust God that you are exactly where you
are meant to be.
May you not forget the infinite possibilities that
are born of faith.
May you use those gifts that you have received,
And pass on the love that has been given to you.
May you be content, knowing you are a child of
God.

Let His presence settle into your inner most being,
And allow your soul the freedom to sing, dance,
and to bask in the Son.
He is there for each and every one of you.

§

Prayer is the most powerful tool we have.

PRAYER BEFORE STARTING WORK

My Heavenly Father,
As I enter this work place, I bring Your presence with me.
I ask Your peace, Your grace, Your mercy, and Your perfect order into this office.

I acknowledge Your power over all that will be spoken, thought upon, decided, and done within these walls.

Lord, I thank You for the gifts You have blessed me with.
I commit to using them responsibly, in Your honour.

Give me a fresh supply of strength to do my job.
Anoint my projects, ideas, and energy, so that even my smallest accomplishment may bring You glory.

Lord, when I am confused, guide me.
When I am weary, energise me.
When I am burned out, infuse me with the light of the Holy Spirit.
May the work that I do and the way I do it bring faith, joy, and a smile to all who I come in contact with today.

And Lord, when I leave this place, give me traveling mercies.

Lord, I thank you for everything You've done, everything You're doing, and everything You're going to do.

In the name of Jesus I pray, with much love and thanksgiving,
Amen.

IN THE NAME OF JESUS

Father, I ask you to bless the one reading this right now.
I am asking You to minister to their spirit at this very moment.

Where there is pain, give them Your peace and mercy.

Where there is self-doubting, release a renewed confidence in Your ability to work through them.

Where there is tiredness or exhaustion, I ask You to give them understanding, patience and strength, as they learn submission to your leading.

Where there is spiritual stagnation, I ask You to renew them by revealing Your nearness, and by drawing them into greater intimacy with You.

Where there is fear, reveal Your love and release to them Your courage.

Where there is a sin blocking them, reveal it and break its hold over their lives.

Bless their finances; give them greater vision and raise up leaders and friends to support and encourage them.

Give each of them discernment to recognise the evil forces around them, and reveal to them the power they have in You to defeat them.

I ask You to do these things in Jesus' name. Amen.

FINANCIAL BLESSING

Heavenly Father,
I pray that You will abundantly bless my family
and me. I know that You recognise that a family is
not just a mother and father, sister and brother,
husband and wife, but all who believe and trust in
You.

Father, I send up a prayer request for a financial
blessing for me and all whom I am acquainted
with. I recognise that the power of joined prayer
from those who believe and trust in You, is more
powerful than anything.

Father, deliver the person reading this right now
from debt and debt burdens.

Release Your godly wisdom that I may be a good
steward over all that You have called me to be. I
know how wonderful and mighty You are and how
if we just obey You and walk in Your Word and
have the faith of a mustard seed, You will pour out
blessings. I thank You now for the recent blessings
I received and for the blessings yet to come,
because I know You are not done with me yet!

I pray this request in Jesus' name,
Amen.

HELP US

Help us to remember that the 'jerk' who cut us off in traffic last night is a single mother, who worked nine hours that day and was rushing home to cook dinner, help with homework, do the laundry and spend a few precious moments with her children.

Help us to remember that the pierced, tattooed, disinterested young man, who can't seem to count change correctly, is a worried, 19-year-old college student, balancing his apprehension over final exams with his fear of not getting his student loans for next semester.

Remind us, Lord, that the scary looking tramp, begging for money from the same spot every day (who really ought to get a job!) is a slave to addictions that we can only imagine in our worst nightmares.

Help us to remember that the old couple walking annoyingly slowly through the store aisles and blocking our shopping progress are savouring this moment, knowing that, based on the biopsy report she got back last week, this will be the last year that they go shopping together.

Heavenly Father, remind us each day that of all the gifts you give us, the greatest gift is love. It is not enough to share that love with those we hold dear.

Open our hearts, not just to those who are close to us, but to all humanity.

Let us be slow to judge and quick to forgive; be patient, empathise and love.

Amen.

DEAR LORD

Bless the people reading this prayer right now.
Keep them strong and help them to do Your will.

When times get tough, Lord, help them to see that
You are walking with them.

Keep your loving arms around them. Protect them
from the seen and unseen dangers that surface on a
daily basis. Keep them safe as they travel the
highways and byways of life.

Most of all, Lord, keep them in remembrance of
You. For You are the one who wakes us up in the
morning and gives us the necessities of life.

All these blessings I ask in your name.

Amen.

A PRAYER FROM THE HEART

O Lord, we have come into this quiet place to
worship you in the beauty of holiness.
But our minds are full of the horror of great
darkness. All through the past week, we have seen
visions of the Apocalypse in our own homes –
terror and destruction of men who can bring down
fire from heaven upon the place beneath – blood
and fire and pillars of smoke. In our ears, above
the lamb-bleat of those who say, "We will do evil
that good may come," we hear the voice of the
Dragon. What can we say, O Lord, upon whom the
ends of the world are come? Only the ancient cry,
"Kyrie Eleeson", Lord have mercy!

Never was there a time when Your peace was in
such short supply in the hearts of men and women.
We pray for the peace of Jerusalem, Your dwelling
place of old, and for the lands of the Middle East
where Jesus walked. O Thou, who causes wars to
cease to the ends of the earth, we pray that you will
dramatically shorten this horrible conflict, that the
hungry may be fed in the desert lands and that the
bread of life, in the knowledge of Jesus Christ, can
go to all nations, and Your kingdom come.

Not least, O Lord, we pray that it may first come in
our own hearts, whose innate selfishness needs the
transforming power of Jesus' selflessness. As we
sense the presence of Your Holy Spirit, we ask for

cleansing from all sin and evil. Sanctify our thought processes and make our study of Your Word today, a force for change to this end. Bless the words of the preacher, that, in the words of Your servant Paul, the righteousness of God without the law may be manifested in our hearts and in this world.

Comfort, we pray You, the hearts of those in our own community who mourn the loss of dear ones – we commend to you those who cry for the tragic death of friends and loved ones. We pray for the children and grandchildren – the young, who often do not comprehend the gravity of the situation. We praise Your name for giving those who pass away rest from all their labours.

Now we ask Your Divine blessing upon every service in this place today, and tomorrow in this community. May the saving grace of Your Son be effectively proclaimed and may Your divine unction be granted, especially to those who have the nurture of our children. As we have the permission of the 'powers that be' to visit the homes and speak for Adventist Missions, may we be willing, more than ever, to back up the efforts of ADRA, especially as our churches in the Middle East will become relief stations for the population. We ask your protection for the churches in Baghdad, Mosul and Kirkuk, and especially in Basra.

O Lord, by the ministration of Your grace, make us, in our homes and hearts, to be "what we pretend to be – may prayer be prayer and praise be heartfelt praise" that the straying may be restored and the light of your eternal truth will shine out in this place.

Hear us in this our prayer, which we ask in the name of Your Son, our Saviour, Jesus Christ the Lord.
Amen.

Prayed by Jack Mahon, former Missionary, in Binfield on 29 March 2003, during the Coalition-Iraq war.

THANK YOU LORD

Dear Lord,
I thank You for this day.
I thank You for my being able to see and to hear.
I'm blessed because You are a forgiving and
understanding God.
You have done so much for me and You keep on
blessing me.

Forgive me this day for I have sinned.
Keep me safe from all harm and danger.
Let me start this day with a new attitude and plenty
of gratitude.
Let me make the best of each and every day and
give my best in all that is put before me.

Clear my mind so that I can hear from You.
Broaden my mind that I can accept all things.
Let me not whine and whimper over things I have
no control over.
Let me continue to see sin through God's eyes and
acknowledge it as evil. And when I sin, let me
repent, confess my wrongdoings and receive the
forgiveness of God.

When this world closes in on me, let me remember
Jesus' example - to slip away and find a quiet
place to pray. It's the best response when I'm
pushed beyond my limits. I know that when I
can't slip away, You listen to my heart.

Continue to use me to do Thy Will.
Continue to bless me that I may be a blessing to others.
Keep me strong, so that I may help the weak and unsaved.
Keep me uplifted, so that I may have words of encouragement for others.

I pray for those that are lost and can't find their way.
I pray for those that are misjudged and misunderstood.
I pray for those who don't know You intimately.
I pray for those who don't believe. But I thank you that I believe.

I believe that God changes people and God changes things.
I pray for all my sisters and brothers; for each and every family member in their households.
I pray for peace, love and joy in their homes, that they are out of debt and all their needs are met.
I pray that every eye that reads this knows there is no problem, circumstance or situation greater than God. Every battle is in His hands for Him to fight.

I pray that these words be received into the hearts of every eye that sees them and every mouth that confesses them willingly.

This is my prayer, in Jesus' name,
Amen.

POEMS

BEAUTIFUL FOOTPRINTS

```
                    Oooo
Some people          (  )
come into our lives  ) /
 and quickly go...  (_ /


        oooO
        (  )    Some people
        \ (     become friends
        \ _)    and stay a while...


Leaving beautiful   Oooo
footprints on our     (  )
hearts...             ) /
                     (_ /


     oooO
     (  )   and we are
     \ (      never
     \ _)   quite the same,
            because we have
               made a good friend!!
```

Yesterday is history.
Tomorrow a mystery.
Today is a gift.
That's why it's called the present!

Live and savour every moment...
...this is not a dress rehearsal!

BIRTHDAY CELEBRATION

Guest of Honour: Jesus Christ

Date: Everyday. Traditionally December 25, but He's always around, twenty-four seven.

Time: Whenever you're ready, please don't be late, though, or you'll miss out on all the fun.

Place: In your heart. He'll meet you there (you'll hear Him knock).

Attire: Come as you are... grubbies are okay. He'll be washing your clothes anyway. He said something about new white robes and crowns for everyone who stays till the end.

Tickets: Admission is free. He's already paid for everyone. (He says we would not have been able to afford it. It cost Him everything He had!)

Refreshments: New wine, bread and a cool drink he calls 'living water', followed by a supper that He promises to be out of this world!

Gift Suggestion: Your heart. He's one of those people who already has everything else. (He's very generous in return, though. Just wait until you see what He has for you.)

Entertainment: Joy, peace, truth, light, life, love, real happiness, and communion with God, forgiveness, miracles, healing, power, eternity in Paradise, and much more! (All rated 'G' so bring your family and friends.)

RSVP: Very important! He must know ahead of time, so that he can reserve a spot for you at the table. Also, he's keeping a list of His friends for future reference. He calls it the 'Lamb's Book of Life'.

"Let us be glad and rejoice, and give honour to him: for the marriage of the Lamb is come, and His wife hath made herself ready.

"And to her was granted that she should be arrayed in fine linen, clean and white: for the fine linen is the righteous of saints. And he saith unto me, Write, Blessed are they which are called unto the marriage supper of the Lamb. And he saith unto me, 'These are the true sayings of God.'

- Revelation 19:7-9

CHURCH SIGNS

Searching for a new look?
Have your faith lifted here!

§

People are like tea bags - you have to put them in
hot water before you know how strong they are.

§

When down in the mouth, remember Jonah.
He came out all right.

§

Fight truth decay - study the Bible daily.

§

How will you spend eternity?
Smoking or Non-smoking?

§

Dusty Bibles lead to Dirty Lives.

§

Come work for the Lord!

The work is hard, the hours are long and the pay is low. But the retirement benefits are out of this world.

§

It is unlikely there'll be a reduction in the wages of sin.

§

Do not wait for the hearse to take you to church.

§

If you're headed in the wrong direction, God allows U-turns.

§

If you don't like the way you were born, try being born again.

§

Looking at the way some people live, they ought to obtain eternal fire insurance soon.

§

This is a ch_ _ ch. What is missing?
U R

§

Forbidden fruit creates many jams.

§

In the dark? Follow the Son.

§

Running low on faith? Stop in for a fill-up.

If you can't sleep, don't count sheep.
Talk to the Shepherd.

§

Jesus is coming!
Don't miss him for the world.

§

People who wait until the eleventh hour to call on
Jesus, die at 10:30.

§

A merry heart doeth good like a medicine.
Proverbs 17:22

DIRECTIONS

Make a right onto Believeth Boulevard.
Keep straight and go through the Green Light,
which is Jesus Christ.

From there, you must turn onto the Bridge of
Faith, which is over troubled water.

When you get off the bridge, make a right turn and
keep straight. You are on the King's Highway –
heaven bound.

Keep going for three miles: one for the Father, one
for the Son, and one for the Holy Spirit.

Then exit off onto Grace Boulevard.

From there, make a right turn on Gospel Lane.
Keep straight and then make another right on
Prayer Boulevard.

As you go on your way, yield not to the traffic on
Temptation Avenue. Also, avoid Sin Street
because it is a dead end. Pass Envy Drive, Have
Avenue, Hypocrisy Street, Gossiping Lane and
Backbiting Boulevard. But you have to go down
Long-suffering Lane, Persecution Boulevard, and
Trials and Tribulations Avenue.

But that's all right, because Victory Boulevard is
straight ahead!

I ASKED GOD

I asked God to take away my pain.

God said, "No. It is not for me to take it away, but for you to give it up."

I asked God to make my handicapped child whole.

God said, "No. Her spirit is whole. Her body is only temporary."

I asked God to grant me patience.

God said, "No. Patience is a by-product of tribulations; it isn't granted, it is earned."

I asked God to give me happiness.

God said, "No. I give you blessings. Happiness is up to you."

I asked God to spare me pain.

God said, "No. Suffering draws you apart from worldly cares and brings you closer to me."

I asked God to make my spirit grow.

God said, "No. You must grow on your own, but I will prune you to make you fruitful."

I asked for all things that I might enjoy life.

God said, "No. I will give you life, so that you may enjoy all things."

I ask God to help me love others, as much as He loves me.

God said, "Ahhhh! Finally, you have the idea."

LET GO ~ LET GOD

As children bring their broken toys for us to mend,
I brought my broken dream to God, because He is
my friend.

But then, instead of leaving Him in peace to work
alone,
I hung around and tried to help with ways that
were my own.

At last I snatched them back and said,
"My God, how can you be so slow?"
He smiled and said, "My child, what could I do?
You NEVER LET GO."

GOD'S WORK

Be ye fishers of men. You catch them – He'll clean them.

Coincidence is when God chooses to remain anonymous.

Don't put a question mark where God put a full stop.

God grades on the cross, not the curve.

God loves everyone, but probably prefers 'fruits of the Spirit' over 'religious nuts!'

He who angers you, controls you!

If God is your co-pilot - swap seats!

Most people want to serve God, but only in an advisory capacity.

Prayer: Don't give God instructions, just report for duty!

You can tell how big a person is by what it takes to discourage them.

The task ahead of us is never as great as the Power behind us.

We don't change the message, the message changes us.

The Will of God will never take you to where the Grace of God will not protect you.

MOTIVATION

There is a curve called Failure
A loop called Confusion
Speed bumps called Friends
Red lights called Family
You will have flats called Jobs.

But, if you have a spare called Determination
An engine called Perseverance
Insurance called Faith
And a driver called Jesus,
You will make it to a place called Success!

TAKE TIME TO PRAY

I knelt to pray, but not for long;
I had too much to do.
I had to hurry and get to work,
For bills would soon be due.

So I knelt and said a hurried prayer,
And jumped up off my knees.
My Christian duty was now done,
My soul could rest at ease.

All day long I had no time
To spread a word of cheer.
No time to speak of Christ to friends;
They'd laugh at me I'd fear.

No time, no time, too much to do,
That was my constant cry.
No time to give to souls in need,
But at last the time, the time to die.

I went before the Lord,
I came, I stood with downcast eyes;
For in His hands, God held a book;
It was the book of life.

God looked into his book and said,
"Your name I cannot find.
I once was going to write it down
But you had no time for Me.

GOD WILL DO THE REST

I asked the Lord to bless you
As I prayed for you today.
To guide you and protect you
As you go along your way.
His love is always with you,
His promises are true;
And when we give Him all our cares,
You know He'll see us through.
So when the road you're travelling on
Seems difficult at best,
Give your problems to the Lord,
And God will do the rest.

THE U IN JESUS

Before U were thought of, or time had begun,
God even stuck U in the name of His Son.

And each time U pray, you'll see that it's true,
You can't spell out JesUs and not include U.

You're a pretty big part of His wonderful name.
For U, He was born; that's why He came.

And His great love for U is the reason He died.
It even takes U to spell crUcified.

Isn't it thrilling and splendidly grand,
He rose from the dead, with U in His plan.

The stones split away, the gold trUmpet blew,
And this word resUrrection is spelled with a U.

When JesUs left earth, at His ascension,
He felt there was one thing He just had to mention:

"Go into the world and tell them it's true:
That I love them all - just like I love U."

So many great people are spelt with a U,
Don't they have a right to know JesUs too?

It all depends now, on what U will do;
He'd like them to know, but it all starts with U.

HE WILL SEE YOU THROUGH

I wish for you...

Comfort on difficult days
Rainbows to follow the clouds
Laughter to kiss your lips
Sunsets to warm your heart
Gentle hugs when spirits sag
Friendships to brighten your being
Beauty for your eyes to see
Confidence for when you doubt
Faith so that you can believe
Courage to know yourself
Patience to accept the truth
And love to complete your life.

A~Z WITH GOD

Although things are not perfect,
Because of trial or pain,
Continue in thanksgiving;
Do not begin to blame.

Even when the times are hard,
Fierce winds are bound to blow,
God is forever able;
Hold on to what you know.

Imagine life without His love;
Joy would cease to be.
Keep thanking Him for all the things
Love imparts to thee.

Move out of 'Camp Complaining.'
No weapon that is known
On earth can yield the power
Praise can do alone.

Quit looking at the future,
Redeem the time at hand.
Start every day with worship,
To 'thank' is a command.

Until we see Him coming,
Victorious in the sky,
We'll run the race with gratitude,
Xalting God most high.

Yes, there'll be good times and yes some will be
bad, but...
Zion waits in glory...where none are ever sad!

WHAT GOD IS A LITTLE LIKE

God is a little like General Electric:
He lights your path.

God is a little like Aspirin:
He works wonders.

God is a little like Hallmark Cards:
He cares enough to send the very best.

God is a little like Persil:
He gets out the stains that others leave behind.

God is a little like VO-5 Hair Spray:
He holds through all kinds of weather.

God is a little like Dove Soap:
He cares, no matter what.

God is a little like a corner shop:
He has everything.

God is a little like Alka Seltzer:
Oh, what a relief He is!

God is a little like Scotch Tape:
You can't see Him but you know He's there!

God is a little like Duracell Batteries:
Nothing can outlast him.

God is a little like your credit card:
Don't leave home without Him!

TRUST GOD

Happy moments, praise God.

Difficult moments, seek God.

Quiet moments, worship God.

Painful moments, trust God.

Every moment, thank God!

Have you ever been just sitting there and all of a sudden you feel like doing something nice for someone you care for? That's God…He talks to you through the Holy Spirit.

Have you ever been down and out and nobody seems to be around for you to talk to? That's God...He wants you to talk to Him.

Have you ever been thinking about somebody that you haven't seen in a long time and then next thing you know you see them or receive a phone call from them? That's God… there is no such thing as coincidence.

Have you ever received something wonderful that you didn't even ask for, like money in the mail, a debt that had mysteriously been cleared, or a voucher to a department store where you had just

seen something you wanted, but couldn't afford?
That's God...He knows the desires of your heart.

Have you ever been in a situation and you had no
clue how it was going to get better, but now you
look back on it... That's God...He passes us
through tribulation, for us to see a brighter day.

TRUST GOD.

THOUGHTS

THOUGHTS FOR TODAY

For all the negative things we have to say to ourselves, God has a positive answer.

You say: It's impossible
God says: All things are possible *(Luke 18:27)*

You say: I'm too tired
God says: I will give you rest *(Matthew 11:28-30)*

You say: Nobody really loves me
God says: I love you *(John 3:16 & John 13:34)*

You say: I can't go on
God says: My grace is sufficient *(2 Corinthians 12:9 & Psalm 91:15)*

You say: I can't figure things out
God says: I will direct your steps *(Proverbs 3:5-6)*

You say: I can't do it
God says: You can do all things *(Philippians 4:13)*

You say: I'm not able
God says: I am able *(2 Corinthians 9:8)*

You say: It's not worth it
God says: It will be worth it *(Roman 8:28)*

You say: I can't forgive myself
God says: I forgive you *(1 John 1:9 & Romans 8:1)*

You say: I can't manage
God says: I will supply all your needs *(Philippians 4:19)*

You say: I'm afraid
God says: I have not given you a spirit of fear *(2 Timothy 1:7)*

You say: I'm always worried and frustrated
God says: Cast all your cares on Me *(1 Peter 5:7)*

You say: I don't have enough faith
God says: I've given everyone a measure of faith *(Romans 12:3)*

You say: I'm not smart enough
God says: I give you wisdom *(1 Corinthians 1:30)*

You say: I feel all alone
God says: I will never leave you or forsake you *(Hebrews 13:5)*

PUMPKIN

A woman was asked by a co-worker, "What is it like to be a Christian?"

The co-worker replied, "It is like being a pumpkin. God picks you from the patch, brings you in, and washes all the dirt off you. Then, he cuts off the top and scoops out all the yucky stuff. He removes the seeds of doubt, hate and greed. And then He carves you a new smiling face and puts His light inside of you, to shine for all the world to see."

GOD IS BIGGER

Stop telling God how big your storm is.
Instead, tell your storm how big your God is.

THROUGH GOD'S EYES

Instead of trying to see God through your circumstances, take the opposite approach. Look at your circumstances through God's eyes.

God does not see your circumstances as insurmountable. He is not intimidated or discouraged by them. Since they aren't problems for him, they shouldn't be for you.

The next time you find yourself looking down in despair, lift your head and start looking up. Stop worrying about your obstacles and start thinking about the God who can help you overcome them.

LIVING AND LANDING

We make a Living by what we get,
We make a Life by what we give.

§

God promises a safe landing, not a calm passage.

PROTECT TODAY

If we fill our hours with regrets of yesterday and
worries of tomorrow, we will have no today in
which to be thankful.

WHAT IF...?

What if God couldn't take the time to bless us today, because we couldn't take the time to thank Him yesterday?

What if God decided to stop leading us tomorrow, because we didn't follow Him today?

What if we never saw another flower bloom, because we grumbled when God sent the rain?

What if God didn't walk with us today, because we failed to recognise it as His day?

What if God took the Bible away tomorrow, because we would not read it today?

What if God took away His message, because we failed to listen to the Messenger?

What if God hadn't sent His only begotten Son, because He wanted us to be prepared to pay the price for sin?

What if the door of the church was closed, because we did not open the doors of our hearts?

What if God stopped loving and caring for us, because we failed to love and care for others?

What if God stopped listening to us, because we would not listen to Him?

What if God answered our prayers the way we answer His call to service?

What if God met our needs the way we give Him our lives?

RULES TO BE HAPPY

God didn't promise days without pain, laughter without sorrow, sun without rain. But, he did promise strength for the day, comfort for the tearful, and light for the way.

Disappointments are like road humps: they slow you down a bit, but you enjoy the smooth road afterwards. Don't stay on the hump too long. Move on!

When you feel down because you didn't get what you wanted, just sit tight and be happy, because God is thinking of something better to give you.

When something happens to you, good or bad, consider what it means. There is a purpose to life's events, to teach you how to laugh more or not to cry too hard.

You can't make someone love you; all you can do is be someone who can be loved. The rest is up to the person, to realise your worth.

The measure of love is when you love without measure. In life there are very rare chances that you will meet the person you love and who loves you in return. So once you have it, don't ever let go, the chance might never come your way again.

It is better to lose your pride to the one you love, than to lose the one you love because of pride. We spend so much time looking for the right person to love or finding fault with those we already love, when, instead, we should be perfecting the love we give.

When you truly care for someone, you don't look for faults, you don't look for answers, you don't look for mistakes. Instead, you fight the mistakes, you accept the faults and you overlook excuses.

Never abandon an old friend. You will never find one who can take his/her place. Friendship is like wine - it gets better as it grows older.

Remember the five simple rules to be happy:
1. Free your heart of hatred.
2. Free your mind from worries.
3. Live simply.
4. Give more.
5. Expect less.

No-one can go back and make a brand new start. Anyone can start from now and make a brand new ending.

FAITH AT WORK

When things get tough, always remember...

Faith doesn't get you around trouble,
it gets you through it!

BIRDS OF A FEATHER...

As you become more sensitive to what is really
important in your life, people who appreciate the
same values, will be drawn to you, and together
your enjoyment of life will be multiplied.

Deepak Chopra

AND JUST IN CASE YOU FORGOT…

If God had a refrigerator, your picture would be on it.

If God had a wallet, your photo would be in it.

He sends you flowers every spring and a sunrise every morning.

When you want to talk, He listens.

He could live anywhere in the Universe and yet He chose your heart.

And that Christmas gift He sent you in Bethlehem?

Face it friend, God is *crazy* about you.

LETTER FROM GOD TO WOMEN

When I created the heavens and the earth, I spoke
them into being.

When I created man, I formed him and breathed
life into his nostrils.

But you, woman, I fashioned after I breathed the
breath of life into man, because your nostrils are so
delicate. I allowed a deep sleep to come over him,
so that I could patiently and perfectly fashion you.

From one bone, I fashioned you. I chose the bone
that protects man's life; I chose the rib, which
protects his heart and lungs and supports him, as
you are meant to do. Around this one bone, I
shaped you, I modelled you. I created you
perfectly and beautifully.

Your characteristics are as the rib: strong yet
delicate and fragile. You provide protection for the
most delicate organ in man, his heart. His heart is
the centre of his being; his lungs hold the breath of
life. The rib cage will allow itself to be broken
before it will allow damage to the heart. Support
man as the rib cage supports the body.

You were not taken from his feet, to be under him,
nor were you taken from his head, to above him.

You were taken from his side, to stand beside him and be held close.

Adam walked with me in the cool of the day, yet he was lonely. He could not see me or touch me. He could only hear me. So everything I wanted Adam to share and experience with me, I fashioned in you; my holiness, my strength, my purity, my love, my protection and support. Man represents my image, woman my emotions.

You are special because you are an extension of me. Together, you represent the totality of God.

DREAMS THAT ALWAYS COME TRUE

When dreams come true at last, there is life and joy.

- Proverbs 13:12

If Solomon is correct, all you need is one dream to come true to get you moving forward. Here are three that always come true:

1. If your dream is to become rich by GIVING, it will always come true. But if your dream is to become rich by getting, you will never get enough - or if you do, you will become poor protecting it. When you give, you are declaring that you have enough to let some go - that means you're rich! On the other hand, if you are too poor to be generous, you will always be poor, because you will never have enough.

2. If your dream is to become happy by HELPING others, it will always come true. When you help others, you are using your power. If you have the power to help, that means you are not helpless, because helping makes you focus on your strength, not your weakness. On the other hand, if your dream is to become happy by using others, you will never be happy, because others can't make you happy, and you will only 'use up' every relationship you have got and keep having to find others.

3. If your dream is to become fearless by TRUSTING God, it will always come true. There is only one way to become fearless: trust in someone that you know will never let you down! David found that out. Listen: "The Lord is my light and my salvation - whom shall I fear? The Lord is the stronghold of my life - of whom shall I be afraid? When my enemies and my foes attack me, they will stumble and fall" (Psalm 27:1-2). What assurance!

You will **never** find anyone or anything more dependable than the Lord!

Bob Gass Ministries
Stoke-On-Trent

CONNECTIONS

'I am too blessed to be stressed!'

§

The shortest distance between a problem and a solution is the distance between your knees and the floor.

§

The one who kneels to the Lord, can stand up to anything.

A CREED TO LIVE BY

Don't undermine your worth by comparing
yourself with others.
It is because we are different that each of us is
special.

Don't set your goals by what other people deem
important.
Only you know what is best for you.

Don't take for granted the things closest to your
heart.
Cling to them as you would your life. For without
them, life is meaningless.

Don't let your life slip through your fingers, by
living in the past or for the future.
By living your life one day at a time, you will live
all the days of your life.

Don't give up when you still have something to
give.
Nothing is really over until the moment you stop
trying.

Don't be afraid to admit that you are less than
perfect.
It is this fragile thread that binds us to each other.

Don't be afraid to encounter risks.
It is by taking chances that we learn how to be
brave.

Don't shut love out of your life by saying it is
impossible to find.
The quickest way to receive love is to give love;
the fastest way to lose love is to hold it too tightly;
and the best way to keep love is to give it wings.

Don't dismiss your dreams.
To be without dreams is to be without hope; to be
without hope is to be without purpose.

Don't run through life so fast that you forget not
only where you have been, but also where you are
going.
Life is not a race, but a journey to be savoured,
each step of the way.

Nancye Sims

OTHER BOOKS BY MANDRA PUBLISHING

Let the Earth Speak of God's Creation
A fresh look at the creation argument, with a good balance between science and Scripture; new info. on dinosaurs. Illustrated. Valuable to anyone with GCSE and above education. *Chapters include*: Origin and Structure of the Earth, …Up and Down the Geological Column, Extraterrestrial Impact..., Cool Runnings…, Taming the T-Rex, The Geological Column and Calvary. *Cost: £6.50*

Spiritual Gifts: Identify and Develop Them
lives up to its title, providing scriptural basis for the identification and development of one's spiritual gifts; and helps the reader to examine new gifts, while facilitating creativity in developing them. *Chapters Include*: The Basic Principle, Definition and Application, Evidence in your Life. *Cost: £5.95*

Sanctified Weakness is more than a collection of inspirational sermons speaking to the heart and mind of young people, or anyone. It is also the story of a life, weak in the flesh, but touched by God. You won't be able to put it down. Chapters include: Chasing Bubbles, Giant Killer, Can't Cook, Won't Cook – Death in the Pot, Keeping it Real, Get a Life, Dream On. *Cost: £5.95*

Orders to: *Mandra Publishing, PO Box 5136, Riseley, RG7 1GT.* (P&P **free** for any two or more books.)